ADVANCE PRAISE

"It troubles me as a developmental psychologist that boys now receive their first sex education from pornography, and that sex industries of all kinds exploit their vulnerability by offering increasingly provocative, dehumanized content. To encourage the humanity of our men and to end gender-based abuse and violence, we must acknowledge how this content shapes the minds, attitudes and behavior of our boys. Jason's courageous and powerful story helps to reveal these truths, and I heartily recommend it to all who wish for a fairer, healthier world."

—MICHAEL C. REICHERT, PhD, author of *How To Raise A Boy: The Power of Connection to Build Good Men*

"As men we unconsciously pursue wealth, power and sex to heal our inner wounds and compensate for our own insecurities. In the process we deny ourselves the love and connection we crave while sabotaging our lives. Jason vulnerably shares his own journey and the true cost of this denial. His courage is both and a wake-up call for men."

—LUCAS KRUMP CO-FOU

SILICON VALLEY PORN STAR

SILICON VALLEY PORN STAR

A MEMOIR OF REDEMPTION AND REDISCOVERING THE SELF

JASON PORTNOY

Hardcover ISBN: 978-1-5445-3213-4
Paperback ISBN: 978-1-5445-3214-1
Ebook ISBN: 978-1-5445-3219-6
Audiobook ISBN: 978-1-5445-3112-0

This book is a memoir. It reflects my present recollection of experiences over time. Conversations are presented with as much fidelity as possible. In some instances, I changed the names and identifying characteristics of individuals. Some of the people I worked with professionally went on to become quite famous. Please don't let my actions cast even the smallest shadow on any of them. They had no idea what I was doing. I kept my secrets well hidden.

For Anne Marie.
You are love.
Thank you.

The true human condition in its most perfect form has no secrets. It does not hide, but exists in clear love.

—GARY ZUKAV, *SEAT OF THE SOUL*

...this identity of mine that liked to look at porn needed a name. "Let's call him Porn Star," Melissa says one day. We both laugh, and the name sticks.

THE WAKE-UP CALL

"Much of your pain is self-chosen. It is the bitter potion by which the physician within you heals your sick self."

—KHALIL GIBRAN, *The Prophet*

FEBRUARY 2015

THE RINGER ON MY PHONE IS LOUD ENOUGH TO WAKE me up, and it scares the shit out of me. It's early on a Saturday morning. I never get calls at this hour, and I don't recognize the number. Something isn't right. My heart races. "Hello?"

"Where is my daughter?"

The woman's voice is raspy, unfamiliar to me. And who is her daughter? I'm confused and groggy. "Uh...who is this?"

"This is Lisa's mother. I know she was with you last night. Where is she?"

Unmistakable anger rises in her voice as she speaks. Fear creeps into my room.

I bolt upright. A sliver of light shines through the drapes and casts a line across the bed, as if pointing to the empty space where my wife usually sleeps. I stare at the vacant side of the bed, awake, yet not quite comprehending what's happening.

Flashing back to the night before, I see myself waiting at the hotel, pacing, repeatedly checking my phone, trying not to get aggravated. Lisa arrived two hours late.

I've become so good at lying by now that I already know what to say: *You have the wrong number. I don't know any Lisa.* But deep inside, I knew I was caught. Denial would just make things worse. Besides, what if something bad really did happen to Lisa?

"I'm sorry." I clear my throat. "I don't know where she is. She told me she was going to a club with friends last night. Maybe check with one of them?"

"*You* are the last person she was with." She distinctly pronounces each syllable, almost in *staccato*. "And now, she is not here. I know where you live, Jason. I know where you work. If something has happened to her, I will find you."

The line goes dead.

A wave of panic comes over me. Fear isn't just in my room now, it has climbed into my bed and fused into every cell in my body. Slowly, the realization that I won't be able to control this sinks in. I have gone too far this time. I know nothing about these people.

I try to slow my breathing, but I can't. I am alone and I am frightened. I stare at my phone, but I don't know what to do with it. I can't tell anyone about this. Nobody.

Actually, there is one person who already knows a lot of my secrets. She's the only person I can be honest with about this, and she'll know how to help me. I send a text message to my life coach: *I'm having an emergency. Can you talk?*

Immediately my brain switches gears. It races to calculate a fix, tries to spin a way to explain things to make them sound less bad than they are. I turn sideways on the bed to open the drapes and let in more light. Outside the world looks distant, like I'm suddenly viewing it from an alternate reality. The silence of the room presses against my ears. *How am I going to get out of this?*

A few minutes later, my cell rings, startling me again. I hope it is my life coach, but it's the unknown number from before.

"Hello?" I try to sound polite.

"Lisa just came home." The woman's voice is low and shaking. She speaks slowly, angrily. "What did you do with her?"

"I didn't do anything with her," I lie.

"That is *not* what she said."

"What did she say?" I ask. *What could she have said?*

"You have defiled her!" She yells the accusation. "She told me everything. She told me what you did to her. She is devastated. She was a *pure* woman. I am going to find you."

I jump out of bed. *What the hell?* This woman is wrong. Granted, I had *wanted* to have sex with Lisa the night before, but she'd said *no*. We fooled around a little, but no sex took place. I certainly hadn't *defiled* her.

"I swear to you." I pace my words, trying to control my shaking voice. "I did not have sex with your daughter."

"I will take her to the doctor, and we will see."

The line goes dead again.

Once more, I stare at my phone, then look out the window, feeling powerless. Already I know Anne Marie will find out about this. She'll be so hurt. *After everything we've been through, how could I do this to her?* Shame washes over me. The room spins.

My breath comes in shorter and shorter. Something wasn't right about any of this, but in slowly dawning dread, I realize how stupid, and possibly dangerous it was to try to do anything with Lisa in the first place. I knew she lived with her mother. She didn't have a car, which created logistical issues when we'd tried to hook up. But really, I knew nothing else about her, except that it was very possible she knew where I lived. That meant her mother could send someone over to beat the shit out of me.

My phone blinks with a text message. My life coach, Melissa. Thank god she is an early riser.

Good morning. Yes, you can call me.

I dial immediately. Yes, please rescue me, I think.

"Hi. What's happening?" Her typically cheery voice has a hint of concern. This is the first time in five years of coaching that I've contacted her with an emergency.

"I'm not exactly sure." I pace the room, staring at the floor. Fear forces words out of me in a rush, faster than my brain can try to fix the situation. "Last night I did something I shouldn't have. I met up with a girl. Anne Marie and Maya are out of town. I swear nothing bad happened, but I just got a call from the girl's mother telling me she is going to come after me. She knows where I work."

Melissa is quiet. I wait in anxious anticipation. I don't expect sympathy from her; that's not her style. She will hold me accountable.

"Where are you right now?" she eventually asks.

"I'm at home." I pause, then add, "I'm scared."

"Do they know where you live?"

"They might. I met Lisa at the gym. She's the receptionist. My address would be in their records, but I don't know if she has access to them."

"I think you need to find out if they have your address."

My brain starts to come back online. Yes, right. Of course. That sounds like a good first step. "I can call the gym. Maybe speak with the owner." My voice trails off. The implications of my words are clear to me immediately: this will not remain a secret.

"That's probably a good idea," Melissa says.

We hang up, and I return to the bed where I sit, motionless, staring out the window. I can't keep living like this. I've known that for a while. The lies have been eating away at me for a long time. It needs to end. All of it.

Knowing that doesn't make it any easier to dial the gym. It is a small local place. I'm not close with the owners, but I know them well enough to say *hello* if we pass in the hallway. And from now on, every time they look at me, they will think about how I hooked up with their receptionist. I feel the embarrassment welling up inside me before anyone even answers the phone.

After a brief moment on hold, I'm connected with one of the owners and I tell her what is happening. Although I fumble my words and don't give her gory details, she learns enough to know I hung out with Lisa last night, and now her mother is threatening to come after me. She listens quietly and, thankfully, keeps the conversation on a professional level.

"Interestingly, Lisa was on the schedule for yesterday and never came in," she says, which surprises me. "She didn't even call out or anything. It's not the first time that's happened, and I was planning to fire her on Monday."

"Oh, wow," was all I could muster. That was a bit of a relief. "But did she have access to membership records? Is it possible she knows my address?"

"No, not to that information. Only your name and photo pop up on the monitor when you check in, so that's all she would see."

"Okay, great, thank you." There is an awkward pause. I feel like I have to say more to fill in the empty space. "Listen, I'm really embarrassed about—"

"We don't need to go there," she interrupts. "Your life isn't any of my business."

"Oh, well, thanks again."

"Just one more thing," she says before we hang up. "You might consider going to the police."

Alarm bells go off in my head. *The police! Hell no!*

I try to sound unfazed. "Why do you say that?".

"I don't think the woman Lisa calls her 'mother' is really her mom," she says. "There's something fishy about them. Be careful."

"Do you think I should be scared?" The fear bubbles up again.

"No, no. I don't think they're dangerous. But if she calls again, think about getting the police involved. I have a feeling that would scare them away."

I thank the owner, and she wishes me luck. As I click off the call, I realize that going to the police isn't such a bad idea after all. I can't tell anyone else about what is happening, and I've committed no crime. If I'm worried about the "mother" coming after me, the police may have good advice.

I decide that I have nothing to lose, Google the local police non-emergency number, and dial it. As I wait for someone to answer, I change my mind. *Calling the police is a terrible idea!* But it's too late—someone answers quickly. Once again, I trip over my words but manage to communicate something; this time it's that I'd like to file a report because someone is harassing me. The woman politely tells me I have to physically go to the station to do it. *Great. Now I have to talk to someone in person about this.*

"I'll let someone know to expect you," she says before we hang up.

I do my best to convince myself not to go to the police station while I dress, but then Lisa's "mother" rings my phone again, and it becomes clear that I need to go.

"Hello?" Somehow, I'm less afraid of her now.

"Lisa is in her room. She is devastated."

After talking to the gym owner and planning to go to the police, I'm suspicious now. Is Lisa *really* devastated? Nothing that crazy happened between us. What could she be *devastated* about? Is this woman *really* her mother? Is this all an act?

"Can I speak to her?"

"NO, YOU CANNOT SPEAK TO HER!" the woman yells. "You are going to pay for this."

My fear rises again. I stand to try escaping the discomfort. I open my mouth, but I'm at a loss for words. *How do I fix this?*

The woman continues: "She will need counseling. It is very expensive. You will pay for it, and anything else she needs."

I am simultaneously relieved and confused. Relieved because "pay for this" means paying money, not me getting beaten up. But I'm confused by "anything else." *What could that mean?*

I grope for the chair in the corner of the bedroom to sit down. Of course I'm disappointed in myself, again, and filled with shame, again. But the fear was giving way to anger. Lisa had been a very willing participant in our tryst. She eagerly agreed to my suggestion a few months ago that "we should hang out sometime." I remember the electricity I felt when I got the first text from her at my Google Voice number, the one I'd set up for communications I didn't want Anne Marie to see.

Hi! It's me. Is it safe to text you here?

She willingly climbed into my car in a mall parking lot a few weeks later, but she would only go so far. The tease, the siren, it drew me in. She happily agreed to meet me at the hotel the night before. She wasn't devastated. And this woman on the phone was not her mother. Meanwhile, I was a rich, white man who...

Disgust landed a nauseating gut punch, adding to the cocktail of emotions already swirling inside me. I am a rich, white man chasing after a pretty, young girl. Lisa's willingness didn't matter. I am a predator. It is my fault this is happening.

Realizing this makes me think the easiest way through the situation might just be to play along.

"I'm sorry to hear that she's devastated." I press my fingertips hard against my forehead. "I will pay for her to get counseling."

"You will pay for whatever she needs," she commands with a hiss. "If you don't, we will come find you."

I let the call remain quiet for a moment, then ask, "How much do you want?"

My chin falls against my chest as the words leave me. I didn't even have the strength to hold my head up anymore. Not only will Anne Marie probably find out about this, but I will also have to spend our family's money to keep my secrets from going public.

"I don't know how much." The woman's voice was somehow a little lighter. "It will be a lot, though. I will know after I take her to the doctor."

"I understand." I lift my head. "You take her to the doctor. I'm going to the police to get advice."

There was a long pause. It felt like hours. Eventually, she says, "You do what you need to do," and hangs up.

* * *

IT IS STILL EARLY ENOUGH that the streets are pretty empty as I make my way to the police station. The gray sky, barren trees, and snow-covered ground tell me it's going to be a cold day. Somehow that seems fitting. Fortunately, my brain has been in fix-it mode for a while, so I'm lost in my head and don't have to feel anything.

That changes when I pull up to the police station. There is a cruiser parked out front, and a policeman gets out as I approach. Suddenly I am very self-conscious, aware that I am pulling up in a BMW. I have done everything the stereotypes about rich, white men have said I would do. I am a walking cliché. My face burns with shame. I feel gross.

I exit my car and the world is a blur. I can barely focus on anything, but the officer is hard to miss. He is six-feet-five-inches tall, bald, and enormous. Thumbs in his belt and sunglasses covering his eyes, it is clear from his body language that he will have no tolerance for small talk or bullshit. Fortunately, he starts the conversation before it is obvious that I have no idea how to.

"How can I help you?" he asks.

The contrast between us can't be any clearer, and I immediately have respect for this man. He is good; I am bad. He commands respect; I pretend like I deserve it. He is a man; I am a boy. At this moment, my "problem" seems petty and stupid compared with the real problems he deals with on a daily basis.

I want his approval. I sense that the only way to earn his respect is to tell the truth concisely. But that's easier said than done; the words felt thick and awkward as I try to speak them.

"Last night I hooked up with the receptionist from my gym."

I pause. He nods but is silent.

"And, uh, this morning I got a call from her mother saying that the girl was upset. I swear I did not do anything wrong with her. We parted on very good terms."

He stands up even taller. I didn't realize that was possible.

I hurry to the punchline. "The mother threatened to come after me and said that I would need to pay money for counseling and 'anything else.' The girl knows where I work and I am afraid that they are going to physically, uh, *harass* me."

"Girl or woman?" he asks.

I swallow. "She's a legal adult."

His face shows no emotion. "Has she made a specific threat against you or your family?"

"No."

"There isn't much we can do unless someone makes a specific threat."

"Uh, what about a financial threat? Is that some kind of extortion?"

"Did she ask you for specific amounts of money?"

"No. She was vague about that. She said she'd call me later to tell me an amount."

He nods, slowly. "My guess is this woman knows that if she keeps her threats vague there is nothing the police can do. It sounds to me like she's done this before. My advice is to stop talking to them. They'll go away and try scamming someone else."

Scamming? Was this a scam? Have I been that naïve?

I come back to reality. "I told the mother I was going to the police," I offer, hoping to sound like I have some ability to manage my own life.

"That should scare them off."

I wasn't sure what to say next. If we were done talking, it meant I had to leave. Back home, probably. Back to being alone. I wasn't ready for that. I wasn't good at being alone.

"Are you going to tell your wife?" he asks, which kind of shocks me.

"Ye-es," I say slowly. "I think I have to."

"Good luck." I notice a tiny smirk and a subtle shake of his head. "I don't envy your situation."

* * *

IT IS STILL CLOUDY, GRAY, and cold when I'm back in my car—alone—making my way home. I'm not sure what to do with myself so I look for busy work. Making the bed, though a small accomplishment, helps me feel a tiny bit more grounded in reality. I sit on the bed staring out the window again, but I don't see anything. Everything is blank. The monkey-brain mind chatter is gone. Finally, I'm numb from feelings. It's like an atomic bomb has gone off inside of me and obliterated everything—until Anne Marie and Maya find their way into the blankness.

In this moment, they are the only things that matter. My work, my car, the money, the women. Suddenly, they all seem so pointless. I want to grasp onto my family but when I try, they disappear. They are not here with me. I am alone in this. My heart aches for them. I almost lost them once before; I can't lose them now. *I must fix this.*

I text Melissa about my trip to the police station and what the officer said and ask if she has time to talk later. She replies that she'll be available in the early afternoon. We confirm two o'clock—just a few hours away, but an eternity.

My phone buzzes with another text message.

Hi sonshine! We are up and we had breakfast and we are ready to start the day. Should we meet you at the house?

Oh my god, my parents. My mother and stepfather, Bill, are in town. I'm supposed to spend the day with them.

I have no desire to pretend that everything is normal, nor do I want to tell my parents what is happening. But hanging out with them means I don't have to be alone while I wait to call Melissa.

They might even be a good distraction for a few hours. I reply: *Good morning! Sure! Unfortunately something has come up and I have a work call at 2pm now, but let's hang out until then.*

I'm in such a state of shock that I move through the next few hours in a sort of trance. By this time in my life, I exist definitively as two different people. As we move around town and have lunch, my parents see the same side of me they normally see, the same side of me that almost everyone else sees. I am fairly cool, calm, and collected. But anyone watching me closely will notice that I am present one minute, then I drift someplace else the next. I am there, but I am not fully there. Part of me is on the other side, in the other place. The place where I fear I might get a secret text message when Anne Marie is looking at my phone because I forgot to silence my Google Voice account. The place where I fear that I may have forgotten to close the porn website when Maya asks to play a game on my laptop. Now it is the place where the angry woman could call me at any moment. The place where, today, I fear that I am going to break Anne Marie's heart and lose my family and be humiliated by the public revelation that a married venture capitalist was hooking up in a hotel room with the receptionist from his gym.

Thankfully, around two o'clock, my parents go back to their time-share to rest for the afternoon. Before we part, my mother reminds me that we have a pottery-making class tonight. I manage to fake a smile, and then tell them I'll pick them up and we'll head over together.

I go back home and retreat, once more, into the master bedroom to have my call with Melissa. I've taken many calls with her while in this room. Normally it feels cozy and safe. But I don't feel cozy and safe today. I feel untethered. I dial her number.

"Hello. How are you doing? Tell me what happened," she says all at once.

I give her more details about my visit to the police station.

"Has the woman called you back?"

"No. I haven't heard from her."

"Okay, good. Maybe she will just go away." She pauses. "Jason, Jason, Jason."

I can't come up with a response, so we are both silent for a minute.

"How did this happen?" she eventually asks.

"I don't know," I start. Then I realize how stupid that sounds. My head falls back against the chair in resignation. "I mean, I do know. This girl and I have been flirting for months. I don't know why I did this. I don't know why I keep sabotaging myself." *Sabotaging myself.* This is the language I've learned after the last incident. "This is worse than what happened a year ago."

"Yes, it is," she agrees.

Again, we are silent for a long while. There is a pattern emerging in my life, and we can both see it now. If I was honest about connecting the dots, I would admit it was a downward spiral. I have been engaging in riskier and riskier behavior. If I continue, I will eventually implode, or self-destruct, just like so many other men I have read about in the media. I don't want that to happen. I have a successful career and a wonderful wife and daughter, both of whom I love deeply. I don't want to lose everything I have worked so hard to build for myself. But when am I going to stop doing these things? I mean *really* stop? Not just for a while, but permanently?

How did I even wind up here anyway? I used to be a normal guy...or at least a normal kid, didn't I?

PART 1

EARLY PROGRAMMING

CHAPTER 1

"The children cry, and their cries are
also the cries of their parents."

—ELDER THADDEUS OF VITOVNICA,
Our Thoughts Determine Our Lives

MARCH 1980

I AM FOUR YEARS OLD AND SQUEALING WITH DELIGHT AS
I jump on a pulled-out sofa bed in my footie pajamas. I'm on a
sugar high because of all the peanut M&Ms I've eaten after dinner.

My mom and her friend Bill are laughing, enjoying my fun.
My sister, Stephanie, five years my senior, is brushing her teeth,
preparing for bed. At this moment, our little two-bedroom apartment is my entire universe. Nothing else exists.

My makeshift trampoline is really my mom's bed. Much
later in life I learned that she slept in the living room because
she could only afford a two-bedroom apartment after her and
my dad divorced, and she had given my sister and me the
bedrooms.

Always the responsible one, Stephanie finishes getting ready for bed and comes to retrieve me. "Time to brush your teeth, Jason."

My sister is my hero, so I grab her hand and follow her lead. Once she gets me situated in bed, my mom arrives, tucks me in, and kisses me goodnight. I am safe and warm and loved, all bundled up in my comforter, and I fall asleep peacefully, as if everything is right with my world. Unfortunately, as time passes, those happy, sweet nights become fewer and fewer.

Just two years later, I'm six years old, sitting on my bed, holding my knees. The screams in the hallway are intensifying. I'm scared. My bed is in the opposite corner of my room from the door, as far away as possible. The headboard is against the wall and I'm suddenly aware that behind the wall there is only the darkness of night.

We now live in the wooded hills of northern New Jersey, close to the border of New York, and there are very few homes around us. Our house is an island in a sea of trees. We are alone out here. I want Stephanie to protect me. Her bedroom used to be right next to mine, but a few months ago she moved to the downstairs bedroom to get further away from the screaming. I'm on my own now.

There's a crash, and something breaks. More screaming. I don't understand what they are fighting about.

"That's it, I'm leaving!" my mom shouts.

Bill yells, "And where the hell do you think you're going?!"

I've heard these lines before, and my body tenses as I wait for my mom's usual response. She delivers it, as if on cue.

"I don't know!" Her voice is frantic. "Maybe I'll just drive off a cliff somewhere!"

The door slams. Outside, the sound of tires speeding off. Then everything is quiet.

I am frozen in fear. Bill's footsteps approach my door. He has never hurt me, but he rages with anger. Instinctively, I know to keep my distance. He turns to enter the master bedroom, across the hall from my room, and slams the door.

I get under my covers. Though I'm relieved the fight is over, I lay on my side and stare at the curtains. Mom will come back, right? She always has before. But...what if this time it's different?

Eventually, I fall into a fitful sleep—alone and scared.

The next day at school I try to pretend like nothing happened the night before, again, but it's getting harder to do that. As I watch the other kids at recess I'm confused. How can they be having so much fun? I desperately want to get lost with them in the games they are playing, but I can't. I hold back, afraid that if I let myself get swept up in the moment, I won't be able to manage the flood of emotions. I have to keep some distance. I have to stay in control.

Protecting myself from feeling pain is something I get good at. By the time I'm seven years old, I've mastered the art of distraction. One day, I sit in the front seat of my father's new car, mesmerized by the headlights that flip up and down. Where do they disappear to? I'm convinced there is magic involved. It is a sun-drenched morning, and I'm surrounded by towering pine trees on the edge of an idyllic lake in New Jersey. The car windows are down and the thick mat of damp brown pine needles on the ground fills my nose with the smell of wet earth. I hear the morning call of birds and the peacefulness of the place touches something inside me. I stare out the front windshield for a while at the lake, then play with the headlights again. My father exits his friend's house and leans into the passenger window, breaking my trance. "Jason, c'mon now, would you please come say 'hi' to Mel?"

"No, I just want to play in the car, Dad."

He hangs his head like he's disappointed or something, but he doesn't force me to go inside. I know he's leaving soon. My mom and Bill got married a few months ago, and now my dad is going somewhere called Illinois, which sounds really far away. So I don't want to go inside and meet his friend; I want to sit in the car with him and be together. Either that or I want him just to leave. I never get to spend much time with him, anyway. Maybe it'd be better if he just wasn't around at all, then I could pretend he didn't exist, and it wouldn't hurt so much.

My dad moves away shortly after that, and the next few years are a bit of a blur. Then something happens around the time I'm nine years old. My mom has two miscarriages that year, and our family seems to go through big emotional swings. It's as if a gray cloud descends to hang over our home. Gradually, I start getting sick more often, and I miss a lot of school. My mom is sick, too. She now takes a pile of pills several times a day. One day she explains to me what each one is for, but there are so many, my head just spins. Our kitchen counter looks like a pharmacy.

During the week, my sister and I are latchkey kids. My mom pays one of the neighbors to pick us up after school and drop us off at home. One sunny fall afternoon, my sister unlocks the door to the house and fixes us a snack of Kraft singles melted on Wonder bread, and I am grateful for her company while we sit at the kitchen table and eat. I love hanging out together and desperately want her to play a game with me, but she just wants to go to her room and talk to her friends on the phone. I beg and I plead, but she is firm in her resolve, so I go outside, dejected, and ride my bike up and down our long driveway and play on the swing set. The forest trees around our yard tower over me; somehow, they make me feel better. Nobody lives near us, so I have no friends nearby to play with, but I've gotten used to being by myself by now.

On rainy days, or in the winter when it is too cold to play outside, I plop on the couch and watch TV shows and movies. It is here that I learn about how to be a man when I grow up. I learn that I need to make a lot of money (or be rich, like a prince) and drive either a Corvette or a Porsche. If I do those things, other guys will like me, and a pretty girl will want to marry me. I will be cool, and I will be happy. This seems like an easy enough formula, so I file it away in my head for later reference.

Eventually, the summer before I start middle school, our family gets a chance at a fresh start when we move down to Hillsborough, New Jersey, in the middle of the state, to be closer to my mom's and Bill's new jobs. No longer an island in a sea of trees, we're in a neighborhood of a quintessential suburb, complete with sidewalks and kids playing in the street. Our new house is so big I get lost as I'm exploring it the first time. The gray cloud hanging over our old house is replaced by sunlight streaming through huge kitchen windows, almost blinding me. Everything is bright and new and exciting. And we have a pool!

That July, my sister has a sweet-sixteen pool party and I have my own birthday pool party a month later. I have no friends in our new town yet, so my mom invites all my classmates from my old school. The sounds of fun and laughter fill the house and warm my soul. It is a new place, a new beginning. I feel safe here.

Unfortunately, the newness wears off rather quickly. My mom seems really tired the next few weeks. By the time school starts, she's sick again. I see her car in the driveway when I get off the bus. I run to the house and burst through the door, excited to tell her about my first day in my new school.

"Mom! Hey, Mom!"

Silence.

A shiver goes through me, and I notice that none of the lights are on in the house. I go back toward the kitchen.

"Mom?"

Nothing.

She must be in her room.

I bound up the stairs with all the energy of a sixth grader and see that her door is closed. I knock. No answer. I open the door slowly. The lights are off, the shades are down, and it is very dark. I tiptoe in and see my mom lying in bed with a towel over her eyes.

"Jason? Is that you?" she asks.

"Hey, Mom." I approach the bed. "Are you okay?"

"I'm not feeling too good," she whispers. She clears her throat and musters enough energy to speak. When she does, her voice is weak. "Why don't you sit with me and tell me about your day?"

I sit on the side of the bed and start telling her about my new school. The bus ride was so fun. The school is huge and there are so many kids. And I have a locker! I tell her the combination, proud that I've remembered it.

"That's really nice, J," she replies. "Can you give me a hug? I need a hug today."

"Sure," I say slowly. For some reason, I'm reluctant. I don't really want to give her a hug. I want her to wake up and get out of bed. I want her to be a normal mom like the other kids' moms.

I dutifully give her a hug, but she is sweaty and lifeless, and I don't want to be close to her. A wave of guilt flows over me and I am confused by my own feelings. My body begins to itch with discomfort. My heart beats faster. I have to go now. I can't stay here.

"I'll come back and check on you later, okay?" I ask.

"Okay." It is barely a whisper. She is almost asleep again.

I quietly exit the room. As soon as the door closes behind me, I race down the stairs and out the front door into the bright afternoon sunshine. My new friends down the street will be starting a game of pickle soon. I run a few houses down to join them, get lost in the game, and forget about what it felt like to be in that room with my mom.

Ever so gradually, it starts to feel like the gray cloud that hung over our old house has found us again. A month later, Bill and I drop my mom off at a place called Carrier Clinic. Mom is going to stay here for a while because she has something called "depression." As the front door swings open, I see smooth linoleum-tiled hallways, low drop-tile ceilings with white fluorescent lighting, and doctors and nurses in white coats pushing people in wheelchairs. I don't really understand why my mom needs to be here. I can't see anything wrong with her on the outside. Why can't she just get out of bed? Maybe these people can help her.

Bill tries to make small talk and comfort me during the fifteen-minute ride home, but I am not in the mood to talk. He had so much anger when I was younger that I've never really felt comfortable with him when my mom isn't around. Now I realize we will be alone together, a lot, and I'm nervous. I know Bill loves me. He has done so much over the years to support both Stephanie and me in school and in all our activities that being nervous to be with him makes me feel guilty. My body feels itchy again. I want to get out of the car.

The house is dark and quiet when we get home, as usual. I go straight to my room where I normally feel safe. Only this time, I don't. I turn on the TV and plop down on my twin bed. Instead of safe, I'm scared and confused about my mom, and I don't like being alone in the house with Bill. Fortunately, one of my favorite shows is on, and I am immediately transported into the action. My body, with all its confusing feelings, gradually melts away, as my awareness is sucked into the screen. I disappear.

* * *

EIGHT MONTHS LATER, A PERFECT summer morning greets me as I roll up the garage door and squint into the daylight. The air is thick from the dew evaporating off the bright green blades of grass in our front yard. Years later, I'd notice that when I visit the East Coast in the summer, the smell takes me back to that place, that time. That pungent, humid summer air was the smell of freedom. Safe in a sea of suburban neighborhoods, I could wander far and wide, away from the gray cloud hanging over our home.

I ride my sister's ten-speed bike to my friend Scott's house. Zipping through the neighborhoods is a newfound freedom, and it is exhilarating. I pedal as fast as I can to see if I can break my speed record.

I met Scott on my spring soccer team, and he became my best friend. We play all day together with only a brief stop for a lunch of sandwiches we make in his kitchen. Both his parents work, but his older brother and sister are around in case we do something dumb and get hurt. We go on long bike rides, attempt skateboard tricks, and play soccer at a nearby field. A wave of sadness hits me every time I see his dad pulling up in the driveway after work, because that is the signal that it's time for me to go.

Slowly I gather my bike and start my ride home. As I round the corner on my street, I see my house, and suddenly I realize my house is once again like a lonely island. Here, in the middle of the neighborhood, it is separate and apart. The rest of the families on our block all know each other, but none of them knows my family. My mom was only at Carrier Clinic for three months last fall, but when she came home, she was so heavily medicated she was barely there. She still hasn't gone back to work. She either sleeps or watches TV or walks around like a zombie in her night-gown with a distant stare on her face.

I feel guilty for not wanting to be at my own house that summer, but that doesn't stop me from leaving every morning. It only makes me confused. Stephanie gets her license that year, and then she's never home either. We never talk about why she's always gone, but we don't have to. We both understand. She doesn't want to be home either.

The next four years of middle school and early high school are mostly the same. I'm a sensitive boy and very self-conscious. I try hard to make new friends and fit in, but it does not come easily for me. I tell myself it's because most of the kids in my new town have been in school together since kindergarten, and that it's hard to break in as a newcomer. Besides, their families are different than mine. Their houses are bright and cheery. My house is dark and scary. But somewhere inside I'm not convinced those are the real reasons, and instead, I increasingly think there is something wrong with me.

I do manage to have at least one good buddy, though, who I hang out with most of the time. First it's Scott, then it's Matt. But despite these solid friendships, I never stop longing to be part of the cool crowd.

As I walk to the school bus each morning, I try on different personas to see if I can find one that will help me fit in. After a few failed attempts at different identities, I learn that mischief is a good way to get attention from my peers, so I become a troublemaker. I flip my teacher the bird one day in class. I light fireworks in my neighborhood after school and engage in other petty nuisances.

Then, seventh grade sees a new constant develop: there is usually a love interest in my life. Over the next four years, I am either entering, in, or exiting an adolescent relationship. Girls are a great distraction from my life at home. Not only that, but

I can create even more drama in my life, get more attention, if I pursue girls who are already in relationships. That pattern of behavior continues through middle school and into high school. Consequently, I spend most of my sophomore year of high school afraid of getting beaten up in school by various girls' boyfriends.

Throughout middle school, soccer feels like my best shot at social redemption, but by the start of high school those hopes are also dashed. I am such a timid player that, instead of charging in after the ball, I'm actually afraid of being part of a play. I fear getting hurt, and that, if I actually got the ball, people would realize I had no idea what to do with it anyway. My freshman year I am the worst player on the team, and frequently the butt of jokes. The other guys are so good, it's as if I'm an outsider on the team. Actually, not "as if." I *am* an outsider. My teammates bond over sports games they watch on TV with their families at night. I can't join the talk—our family doesn't watch sports together at night. Our family doesn't really do much together at all. The other guys seem so confident. I am definitely not confident. I can't shake the feeling I don't belong here either.

When Stephanie is home, we are buddies, but really, she is never around. I miss her so much that I go in her room and play CDs on her stereo, so it feels like she's there. The sounds of her music collection fill the upstairs of the house and help me feel less alone while I'm at my desk doing homework.

Bill works a lot. I sometimes wonder if he is escaping, too. My mom, well, she's still in bed. She sleeps so much that, when I go to my ten-year high school reunion many years later, I'm greeted at the reception table by an old friend shouting, "Hey Portnoy! Did your mom get out of bed yet?!"

I begin high school with a mix of As and Bs, but gradually my grades trend to Bs and Cs, and my attitude declines with them.

At every parent-teacher meeting, my teachers say, "Jason is not working up to his potential." By the time I'm a sophomore, my only response rings loud in my head: *Fuck them. They have no idea.* My teenage self senses a new emotion settling in somewhere, one I'm not familiar with: anger.

Gone are the days when I felt bad for my mom and worried and scared for her. Now when I'm home I feel angry and helpless. *What the fuck, Mom? No, I don't want to sit in your dark room and give you a hug. I hate that we can't ever do anything as a family because you always cancel at the last minute because you don't feel well. Just get the fuck up already! Enough of this!*

But those internal tirades are quickly overtaken by guilt and confusion, and then I bury the whole mess. Eventually, I push the feelings so deep inside me, it will be three full decades before I realize they are buried down there.

By the end of my sophomore year, I find a group of guys I feel like I fit in with. We spend most of that summer drinking beer, smoking pot, and riding mopeds to gas stations to buy cigarettes. I don't really care what I'm doing; I just don't want to be home.

We are comrades in mischief now too, and things escalate. By that fall we are sneaking out in the middle of the night to roam the neighborhoods and steal radar detectors from unlocked cars. One night some of the guys steal an older kid's moped, and that weekend we all take turns destroying it with a sledgehammer at a nearby construction site. I come home with a huge, brand-new boom-box one day, and my parents believe me when I tell them someone gave it to me because I won a bet. Are they that naïve? Don't they know I am burning incense in my room and leaving my window open to cover up the smell of pot and cigarettes? Why don't they stop me?

I'm crying out for help, but they don't hear me. Every beer, every cigarette, every bowl of weed is a plea for help. I desperately want someone to pay attention to me. To stop me from hurting myself. Fortunately, I take things far enough at the start of my junior year to get noticed.

CHAPTER 2

"Mothers play an important part in the masculinizing drama."

—MICHAEL C. REICHERT, PhD, *How to Raise a Boy*

OCTOBER 1992

IT IS A BEAUTIFUL, SUNNY FALL DAY NEAR THE START OF my junior year in high school. My morning classes roll by per usual. I zone out in English class, stare out the window at a cluster of trees. A loud ringing jolts me back to the room. Fire drill!

Soon, the entire student body is milling about on the lawns around the school. A friend and I decide it's the perfect time to finalize a transaction we'd arranged, so we head around behind the gym where nobody can see us. He pulls some cash out of his pocket; I produce a few dime bags from mine. A teacher exits the gym door and...busted. We stand frozen, like two deer in headlights. There's no question: I am fucked.

I spend the next few hours in wood-paneled offices telling my side of the story to various adults. I was selling some pot to my friend, but they say I was "dealing drugs," which sounds so much worse. Eventually my mom enters to retrieve me. *What?* My heart jumps. *She got out of bed for this? She got out of bed for me?* Somehow it feels like everything will be okay now. My mom is going to take care of me. She will know how to fix this.

After a few days spent waiting at home, we hear the decision of the school administrators and police. My mom takes the call. I watch her and wait. Soon, her eyes widen, and the blood drains out of her face. I get tunnel vision as she relays the information to me: the school plans to expel me, and the police plan to send me to a juvenile detention center. I interpret the news as almost life-ending—like I'm destined to be a criminal forever. I don't know what kind of life I was expecting for myself, but this was *definitely* not it.

My mom swings into full counterattack mode, which includes sending me for psychiatric evaluations. After myriad meetings that I am barred from attending, the adults settle on a new sentence for me: a three-month suspension from school, weekly drug counseling, and something that sounds like a billion hours of community service. It is not ideal, but it is manageable.

A month later I sit at the picnic table on our screen porch behind my house, finishing my homework before my tutor arrives. I have grown to love doing my homework out here. The birds are singing, and the occasional breeze ruffles my papers. Something about being in this sun-drenched, airy wooden box soothes me. I sit up straight and well with pride as I put a box around the answer to a complicated physics problem. The antics from my recent past feel like a sideshow all of a sudden. *What was I doing stealing radar detectors and selling pot? That's not me. This is me.*

My life is very simple now. No school. No soccer practices. No hanging out with friends. No homecoming dance with my girlfriend. Instead, I am home all day with my mom, doing homework or getting tutored in my core subjects by teachers from my school. A few evenings a week, I work at a frozen yogurt shop to make money to pay my legal bills.

My mom. My mom! She's awake! She's here! My incident must have shaken her up a little too. Every week, we spend countless hours together driving around: lawyer meetings, court hearings, drug counseling, community service, grocery shopping, and shuttling me to/from work. In the car, she lets me blast Metallica, my favorite band. I crack up one sunny afternoon when she starts singing along to *Master of Puppets*. My mom and I, we are buddies now. She's back. I feel something warm expanding outward from my heart and filling my body, pushing out the darkness that had started taking root there. It is joy. It is relief. I'm not alone anymore. I drum loudly on the dashboard to accompany her singing.

Flyers from colleges stuff our mailbox; it will be time to start applying soon. One day in the car, my mom talks to me about my future. My mom and I haven't had a deep conversation in years, and I hadn't really thought about my future before. We talk about the importance of getting good grades, so I can get into a good college, so I can get a good job afterward. I recall from the early programming I got from TV that if I want to be a man, I have to make a lot of money, so her advice immediately seems right and obvious.

My mother, Bill, and even my biological father are all chemists, and I've enjoyed my chemistry classes so far. Because I like math too, my dad suggests I consider chemical engineering as a college major: a blending of the two subjects. That's funny, I think. I thought engineers drove trains. Regardless, I look up "chemical engineers" in a magazine list, and I see they have the highest starting salaries of any college graduates the prior year. That settles the question. Clearly this is the right major for me.

Winter arrives, and in January I'm allowed to attend school again. For the first few months I feel distant as I move around the halls and attend my classes. The place and the people are the same, but I have changed. I feel like an observer now. I can't quite put my finger on what feels so different to me, but that changes one day in the spring as I file out of the track-and-field locker room with a bunch of guys after a tough practice. Though physically exhausted, as I look at the school building across the parking lot, I am energized by a wave of appreciation for the place and all the adults inside. We don't appreciate what we have until it is taken away from us, and the three months of suspension last fall have humbled me. I now realize this thing they call school is a gift to us kids. I should not take it for granted.

My mom usually picks me up after practice, but she can't today, and I forgot to arrange another ride. My friend Dave introduces me to his friend Kelly, who happens to live very close to me, and she offers to give me a ride. I climb into her BMW and...wow! Immediately I am self-conscious. I've never been in a BMW before, let alone in a nice car with a girl as pretty as Kelly. She is tan and has that relaxed air of a senior in her final semester. She knows who she is, and her confidence makes me realize that I still don't know who I am, and I don't know who I'm supposed to be in this moment. I squirm in my seat.

Fortunately, Kelly turns on some music and makes small talk to fill the space. Our conversation is easy. She is bright and warm. After that day, she drives me home a few times a week, and before we know it, she picks me up on hot spring evenings to go get ice cream. Our relationship blooms from there, and Kelly becomes my first real love.

Kelly is a dedicated student and a gifted athlete. She has her sights set on running at a division-one university where she has already been admitted. She is insanely disciplined and a big ball of positive energy, and she becomes a role model for me. Discipline. Focus. Integrity. These are the pillars of her life, and they are new concepts for me. I try to keep pace with her, to match her stride. I learn a lot from her in the process, and I start to gain confidence in who I am too.

My mom is a lot better now, and she and Bill take advantage of that by getting more active. During the week, they have choir practices in far-flung towns until late in the evening, and many weekends they are gone to stay at Bill's old house near the border of New York. In the summer they are gone for a week at a time. Kelly jokes that she'll call DYFS—New Jersey's Division of Youth and Family Services in those days—to report them for child abandonment. But I'm still so accustomed to being alone that I don't really get her joke. I just thought this was normal.

That summer and into my senior year, I finally settle in with a healthy group of friends, and they become my family. I develop a great friendship with a guy named Mike, and we have a ton of good, clean fun together. Kelly is off at college, and we keep our relationship going with care packages and long, late-night talks on the phone. Now and then, my friends and I drink a little beer, but we are fairly tame about it. Mostly we are good kids, trying to get good grades and prepare for college while still milking some fun out of our last year in high school. In the spring of my senior year, I get an acceptance letter from the University of Colorado, my first-choice school, and I head off to Boulder in the fall for my first semester of college.

* * *

IT IS A FEW MONTHS later, on a clear and cold October night, and I find myself sitting on the back steps of the Folsom Field football stadium with a girl named Anne Marie, talking about our childhoods and our parents. We are high at the top of a hill, but I am so transfixed on her and our conversation that I hardly notice the beautiful twinkling lights of Boulder spread out behind her. She is the only thing that exists in this moment, and her energy envelops me.

We were introduced by a mutual friend a few weeks ago, and we've been inseparable ever since. I still care for Kelly, but it's been over a year since she first left for college, and I've found it increasingly difficult to be in a long-distance relationship. I feel conflicted about what is happening, but Anne Marie is like nothing I've ever experienced, and I can't resist. We are opposites in so many ways. I'm an engineering major; she is studying film. I am New Jersey and Metallica; she is Guam and Natalie Merchant. I am comfortable when I'm busy and moving; she is comfortable sitting still. I am rough around the edges while she seems to float over the earth. Every ounce of her radiates pure love, and everyone she interacts with loves her in return. I am so powerfully drawn to her that nothing else really seems to matter.

Anne Marie also has a boyfriend back home, but by spring semester we've both severed our old ties, and for the next few years my entire world is a blur of Anne Marie, schoolwork, and track-and-field. I bounce around campus with a spring in my step. Boulder is famously sunny over 300 days a year, and I feel like I'm in paradise. The difficult years I experienced in middle school and early high school seem like a distant memory, and I'm on top of the world.

After my suspension in high school, I still have this attitude that education is not something to take for granted, so I bury myself in my studies to show I appreciate the financial sacrifices my parents make to cover my tuition. My GPA reflects my efforts, and I'm proud to hold up my end of the bargain. I barely keep up with the guys on the track team, but they inspire me, and I work my ass off to try to compensate for my lack of ability. I help Anne Marie get through her economics and math classes, and she teaches me how to be a better human. We spend every possible minute together, and as we do, we realize the differences that first attracted us belie a much deeper and more textured commonality.

Anne Marie's mother moved far away—from Guam to California—when Anne Marie was only two years old, mirroring the way my father moved away when I was a boy. Of course, her mom had good reasons, just like my dad, but nevertheless, one of our primary caregivers had left us when we were young. Also, similar to my mother's depression, her father battled alcoholism and drug addiction throughout much of her childhood. She, too, had grown up with a parent who was there, but not always *there*. She, too, had grown up in a house that had secrets from the outside world, and where the center of attention seemed to revolve around one of the parents. She had also felt different from her peers and had experimented with different identities by the time she'd gone off to college, like how I went from dabbling as a petty thief in my early youth to pot-smoker-partier to focused student and athlete. She even went through a life-altering experience late in high school, just like I had. The circumstances of her event were different than mine (she wasn't busted as part of a drug deal at school), but the effect was almost identical: she'd been forced to wake up a little. She had to change course. She had to start figuring out who she was.

Sharing our stories and finding these similarities gives us comfort, and maybe the thing we each crave more than anything else: a sense of belonging. Where before we each felt different from everyone else, now we've found someone just like ourselves. Our bond deepens quickly, and it isn't long before we feel like we are best friends and soul mates, destined to be together forever.

Our relationship becomes very intense. We float through the next few years in our own little bubble, convinced that we are different from everyone else. In fact, it is so intense that sometime toward the end of our third year of college, Anne Marie decides that we need to break up because our relationship is suffocating her. I don't quite understand and can't process it fully. *Am I needy? Do I really require that much attention?*

We settle into an on-again, off-again rhythm. When we are off, I prefer to focus on trying to get dates instead of feeling what it feels like to be alone with myself. I don't like to be alone. I was alone for most of my childhood, and it didn't feel good.

Over time I realize the answer to my question is "Yes, I am needy." I need a lot of attention. This is a difficult blow to my ego, and very disorienting. Perhaps in an effort to gain some independence, I study abroad in Australia for the first semester of my fourth year. But changing locations doesn't change a person, and I need a lot of attention there too.

Anne Marie and I each take five years to finish our degrees, and by the time we graduate we have been on and off for nearly two-and-a-half years. She dated other people during our off times as well, although I don't think it's because she needed to. She was comfortable being on her own, but she was an amazing catch, and never had a shortage of suitors trying to woo her.

In some weird way, our repeated relationship oscillations ultimately bring us closer together. Maybe we had to experience other people to understand what we have with each other. Maybe we really are soul mates. We don't fully know what we are, but by the time we approach graduation at the end of our fifth year, we feel like we are best friends. I get accepted to several different graduate school programs, and when Anne Marie decides she is going to live with her family in Silicon Valley after graduation, I choose Stanford for grad school so I can be close to her.

* * *

I DON'T BELONG HERE.

The professor pushes a chalkboard full of equations up and out of the way, revealing a fresh green canvas for himself. The hieroglyphics continue to flow out of his tiny piece of chalk, and I struggle to keep up with him. Actually, he lost me about ten minutes ago and I have no idea what he's talking about now. I look around the lecture hall from my seat near the middle, and everyone else is nodding along with him and scribbling their own notes.

Shit. I definitely *don't belong here.*

Going to Stanford for graduate school is like going to the Olympics of education. I am surrounded by some of the best and brightest students from all over the world. In Colorado, I graduated with high distinction, near the top of my class. Here I struggle just to keep up.

After high school and college, I know what to do. I know the formula. *Just put your head down, do the assignments and hustle, and you will get through this.* Once again, my life gets very simple, very quickly. After a Jamba Juice breakfast at the student union, my days are classes and reading and homework. Friday and Saturday nights I check IDs at the Arrillaga gym on campus so I can start repaying the student loans I took out to come here. Those shifts pay time-and-a-half because nobody wants them, and I welcome the extra cash.

Anne Marie visits me a few times a week, and we stroll around campus or grab a coffee. We're still not exactly sure what we are, but we enjoy spending time together, and we are comfortable with the lack of clarity in our relationship.

I make some great friends in my degree program, and I notice that most of them had jobs for a few years before they started grad school. Whether it was investment banking, consulting, or helping to run a family business, while I was learning things in an abstract and academic way, they were able to put the classroom material in the context of real-world situations. I see how this benefits them, and I decide that I need to get some real-world work experience too.

I sign up for a newsletter through BASES, the Business Association of Stanford Engineering Students, and it's not long before job postings appear in my inbox. It's fall 1999, and the first internet boom in Silicon Valley is in full swing. New technology startups, awash with fresh millions from venture capitalists on nearby Sand Hill Road, are recruiting feverishly. One of the postings is from a company named Confinity. They are combining the latest wireless communications technology with cryptography so that people can send money to each other using the Palm Pilot VII (the first Palm Pilot to have wireless communications). They are looking for a student who can help with financial analysis on a part-time basis. *I can do that.* With a few mouse clicks, my resume makes its way to them over the internet.

* * *

KNOCK, KNOCK, KNOCK.

It is a chilly December evening and I bounce up and down to stay warm while I wait. Before long, my friend Henrik answers his door.

"Hey Jason, what's happening?" He is his typical warm and jovial self. I love this guy. We live across the way from each other in Escondido Village, a housing community on Stanford's campus. Over the last few months, he has graciously invited me into his social circle so I can make more friends at school. He is getting his PhD in Computer Science and is an expert at the latest wireless communications tech. I can't think of a better person to help me prepare for my interview tomorrow.

"I need your advice on something."

"Sure, sure. Come on in."

"I have a job interview tomorrow with the CEO of a company called Confinity," I tell him once I'm inside. "I need to learn more about wireless stuff, and I have no idea what to wear."

"Oh man, that's awesome! Where is your interview?"

"We're meeting for breakfast at Hobees."

"And what's the CEO's name?"

I think back to the email I got from the company. "Peter... Peter Thiel, I think."

"I've heard that name." Henrik leans back in his chair and stares at the ceiling. "Wait, what was the name of the company again?"

"Confinity. They have a payment service called PayPa—"

"Wait here!" he yells and jumps out of his chair. He runs up the stairs and bounds back down a minute later with a T-shirt.

"Wear this!" He throws the shirt at me.

I hold it up. Surprisingly, it is a Confinity T-shirt, complete with a PayPal.com logo and slogan on the back.

"Oh my god, that's excellent! Where did you get this?!"

"I was at a computer science conference today. They had a booth, and they were handing them out. You should *totally* wear it to your interview. The CEO will love it!"

"Are you sure?" I have no idea what I'm going to wear to the interview, but a T-shirt is not even on the list of things I am considering.

"Yes." He says with his characteristic confidence. "Trust me! It's going to be great."

The following morning, I get up, don my Confinity T-shirt and a jacket, and head off on my bicycle with two copies of my resume in my backpack, carefully printed on special thick paper I'd selected at the campus store. Having never met a CEO, I wasn't sure who I would be looking for once I arrived. Would he be old with gray hair? Wearing a suit? Did I make the right decision to wear the T-shirt?

It turns out I didn't have to worry about identifying the CEO; he spotted me the moment I walked in.

"Jason?" a man asks.

"Yes."

"Hi, I'm Peter," he says cheerfully. "It's nice to meet you. Thanks for coming to breakfast."

We follow the hostess to our table. *Wow, this is not what I expected. This guy is so nice. And he's young. And so casually dressed.* I'm still nervous, but I try to relax as we get settled into our seats.

When I take off my jacket, Peter loves that I am wearing the Confinity T-shirt. He must sense that I'm nervous because he seems to go out of his way to help me feel comfortable. He tells me a little bit about his background, then talks about how and why Confinity was started, and the vision for its future. Then he asks me questions about myself. He is very interested in my background, where I grew up, and what coursework I found most interesting at CU and now at Stanford. At some point I mention in passing that I read a bunch of classic books the prior summer, and that turns out to be what interests him most. He wants to know which books I read, and what I learned from them, and the book list becomes the center of our conversation for the remainder of breakfast. He never even asks for my resume.

Apparently, I had read the right books, because that afternoon I receive an email from someone at Confinity congratulating me and inviting me in for more interviews. A month later, I begin my three-year experience at the company that will later become PayPal. My life would never be the same.

CHAPTER 3

"What does it profit a man, rich or poor, to gain the whole world if he suffers the loss of his soul?"

—THOMAS DUBAY, *Happy Are You Poor*

JANUARY 2000

17,231...*BLINK*...17,234...*BLINK*...17,238...

Confinity's "World Domination Index" blinks on my computer monitor as a group of us return from lunch. I hear someone yell from across the small room of gray cubicles. "Hey look, we got seventy-five new users while we were at lunch!" Shouts of "woohoo!" and "yeah!" rise from the rest of the cubicles, a chorus of jubilation. I've only been working here part-time for a week, but it is a warm and inviting group, and I already feel like part of something special. The people in this group are like the friends I had late in high school. They are sensitive and quirky; smart and determined.

In my first month, the company receives another $23 million of venture capital investment, this time from Idealab and Goldman

Sachs. The pace of user signups only accelerates, and by February we can all feel the momentum building. I drop out of Stanford to work at Confinity full-time, a decision that turns out to be the equivalent of strapping myself to a rocket just as it is lifting off. The trajectory of my life changes forever.

To say things moved quickly during my time at Confinity is a gross understatement. The company goes from having 14,000 users when I start to completing an initial public offering (IPO) only twenty-five months later, in February 2002, a milestone that values the company at roughly $800 million. Along the way, the company goes through a merger with X.com (an online bank started and run by Elon Musk), various additional rounds of financing, several CEOs, at least two name changes, and repeatedly courts acquisition interest from major banks. Ultimately the online auction site eBay, itself experiencing rapid growth, announces it is acquiring PayPal for $1.5 billion in July 2002, almost doubling the company's valuation only five months after the IPO. Even more impressively, all of this happens against the backdrop of PayPal fighting daily for its survival against financial fraudsters and banking regulators. The constant twists and turns galvanize the company culture, and from my vantage point we are one big family, braving the seas against an entrenched financial establishment.

Fortunately, I have a fantastic manager throughout all the growth, Roelof Botha, who makes sure I get a front-row seat to many of the most exciting things happening at the company. By the time eBay completes its acquisition of PayPal in October 2002, just a few months shy of my third anniversary at the company, I am the Vice President of Financial Planning and Analysis. Our team is responsible for reporting companywide performance metrics, and then uses that data to build sophisticated forecasting models to help various other teams plan for the quarters and years ahead. I learn an incredible amount during those years, and I work closely with a lot of extraordinarily talented people. Many of them leave after the eBay acquisition and go on to found other iconic technology companies including YouTube, LinkedIn, Yelp, Yammer, Palantir Technologies, Tesla, SpaceX and, more recently, Affirm. In fact, PayPal's diaspora would later become legendary, earning the nickname "PayPal Mafia."

Not only do I learn a lot and work with amazing people, my stock options become quite valuable as PayPal grows. I don't make millions like the founders and senior employees, but I accrue more wealth than I ever imagined I'd make in my entire life. The first thing I do with the money is pay off my Stanford student loans. Then I buy my first house, in Mountain View, California, just a short drive to PayPal's new office.

As I watch my net worth grow, my confidence grows as well—or maybe it is my ego. I check off the first requirement for being a real man: make a lot of money. Now it's time to work on the car and the woman.

* * *

SEPTEMBER 2002

It is a chilly autumn morning, and Anne Marie and I are crunching through freshly fallen leaves at Chautauqua Park in Boulder, Colorado. At some point in my early years at PayPal, after several years of just being friends, Anne Marie and I had come back together as a couple. Shortly afterward she moved to Los Angeles to pursue a career in film, which was fine for us because

I worked so many hours at PayPal that I had no time to hang out during the week anyway. We visited each other on the weekends and, in general, we made the best of the situation.

After eBay acquired PayPal, things got a little less intense for me at work, so I suggested that we meet in Boulder for one of our weekends together, just to change things up. "Sure!" she had said. She was always up for an adventure.

We make our way up a trail that is familiar to us. Looking back over our shoulders, we realize the horizon is glowing, so we hurry to get to the right spot, our rock, where we plan to sit side-by-side to watch the sunrise. We laugh and reminisce about our college years as we go.

"Remember that time...?" one of us asks. "Oh my god, that was hilarious!" the other answers. We are each in our mid-twenties, so at this point, we've lived through a third of our lives together. We have been lovers. We have been friends. We have laughed, we have cried, and we've been partners for each other during so many life transitions that happen during college and the years that follow. There is a knowing and a depth of understanding that feels like it transcends any words we might exchange. Yet despite all of that, on this particular morning, my stomach is doing somersaults. As we turn to face the horizon and take our seats, I am so nervous I struggle to stay present in our conversation.

Sitting here, on this same rock, is where I first asked Anne Marie if I could kiss her on our first date almost exactly eight years earlier. She had said no that night. Hopefully I'll have better luck this time.

After everything we have been through over the years, I know what I want. But I'm not sure if she wants the same thing. I was ready for this a few years ago, but she had signaled, in her typically graceful ways, that she wasn't ready yet. Yet despite my uncertainty, something is pushing me. Or maybe it is pulling me. Either way, I can't wait any longer. I've gotten my education. I've started a successful career. I've made some money. I bought a house. Brick by brick I am laying the foundations for my life. I want to have a partner by my side for the journey ahead, and by now I know that I will never meet another woman who can even come close to Anne Marie.

While on the outside I feel the early markings of manhood, on the inside I understand that I am still very much a boy. Anne Marie, on the other hand, is far more mature. Her depth and wisdom and grace can reach right into a person's soul and comfort their pain. It's why everyone she interacts with wants to be around her. She makes them feel safe and good and loved. I feel these things too. Her courage inspires me, and I love the fierceness of her spirit. In her I see the traits I so desperately wish to have in myself, or at least in my life. A blending of our energies feels like the perfect compliment.

As the sun crests the horizon, I stand, turn around, and get down on one knee. The look on Anne Marie's face tells me she wasn't expecting this. My confidence wavers. *Have I misread all the cues? How could she not be expecting this?* But there is no time to consider these questions. The ring box is in my hands now. There is too much momentum.

I have never felt this vulnerable in my life. I swallow hard, as if that will hold the feelings at bay.

I open the box to display the ring, tell her how much I love her, and ask if she will marry me.

She looks in my eyes and says, "Yes!"

In that moment I'm not sure if it is her or her sense of adventure that is saying *yes*, but it doesn't matter. Maybe there is too much momentum for both of us. Whatever the case, we are doing this.

We kiss. We hug. We melt into each other. The sun is up now. It is a new day for the world, and the beginning of a new chapter for us.

* * *

IT IS MID-MORNING ON A Saturday in August, eleven months after Anne Marie and I got engaged. San Francisco's famous fog is still thick in the financial district as I walk my short commute—one city block—to the office. Anne Marie and I moved into a nearby high-rise earlier this year when we both started new jobs, and we've been enjoying city life together.

The elevator door opens to the forty-second floor, and as I enter the firm's space, I see Peter through the glass wall of his office. He looks up from the magazine he's reading on his desk, gives me a wave, and then turns to his Bloomberg screen. I don't mind that he doesn't want to chat because I'm just here to finish up some reports I couldn't get done yesterday, and then I need to head up to Healdsburg to meet Anne Marie. She drove up there last night to visit her family for the weekend and continue our wedding planning at the winery. The big day is only two months away.

Wedding planning. Thank god she's focused on it, because I am definitely not. I've been so busy at work that I haven't had time to think about anything else. In fact, the joke between us is that Anne Marie is planning *her* wedding and *I* just happen to be on the invite list. It's kind of funny, but it kind of isn't. Anytime the joke comes out, our laughter is uneasy. I can sense her disappointment over my lack of effort, and I feel guilty that I'm not doing more to help. I comfort my guilt by hiding behind gender stereotypes that I've learned from TV and movies and society over the years. *It's really the bride's day. I'm working hard to make money to pay for it. That's the man's role, right?* I hear another voice inside soothing me. *Yes, Jason. You are doing all the right things.*

I bury the thoughts, wake up my computer, and get to work.

I am the Chief Financial Officer at Clarium Capital, Peter Thiel's hedge fund. Shortly after eBay acquired PayPal, most of the PayPal executive team dispersed. I think Peter was the first to leave. He was thirty-five at the time, with aspirations to be a billionaire by age forty. After PayPal he was off to a good start, but he has a lot of ground to cover in five short years, and the clock is ticking.

Six of us from PayPal followed him to Clarium, and together with a few business friends from his life prior to PayPal, we set out to help him build his vision. Right at the start he does two things that, over time, I learn are hallmarks of his playbook: he gives us all titles and levels of responsibility that reflect our potential, not our current ability, and he implements a generous compensation strategy that tightly aligns our interests with his. His strategies work, and all of us work around the clock to build momentum. Nobody works harder than Peter.

Reports done, I wave to Peter and head to the parking garage. A Ferrari is waiting there to take me on the sixty-minute drive up highway 101 to meet Anne Marie. My car is a 1985 308 GTSi, fiery red with a tan interior and in pristine condition. It is the same exact car Tom Selleck taught me was so cool as I watched him in Magnum PI, one of my favorite childhood TV shows. It cost me $35,000, and that's still a lot of money for me, so I cherish the thing.

The bright red paint lures me as I approach. Once inside, the smell of aged Italian leather envelops me, pulling me deeper into my seat. It is more than a car; it is an assault on all of my senses.

I pick my way through the city, then barrel over the Golden Gate bridge, the engine growling loudly behind me. Soon I hit that spot in Marin where the San Francisco fog capitulates, and the California sunshine streams down through the blue sky. I am transported. I have arrived. I have the money, I have the girl, and I have the car. Everything is perfect.

* * *

IT'S THE BIG DAY. I can't tell if I'm nervous, or scared, or excited. Or maybe I'm all of those things. Or maybe I'm an imposter. Dressed up in this rented tuxedo, I'm supposed to be a man, ready to accept his bride so we can begin a new life together. But I don't feel like a man. How can that be? I'm doing everything they said I'm supposed to. When will I feel like a man?

I look around and I'm amazed at the caliber of the event. Every detail has been planned meticulously. I struggle to take it all in. Then I hear music somewhere and I'm brought back to the moment. Anne Marie appears at the far end of the aisle, her father on one arm, her stepfather on the other. She is so radiant that time stands still for a moment, and suddenly I see her in a way I've never seen her in nine years. She is a queen. She knows so much, and her grace holds so much space, that she carries me and all 200 of our wedding guests. As she glides up to the altar, a wave of dread falls over me and I feel myself fidgeting. I am not yet exactly sure what I am, but I know that I'm not a king. I am not worthy of this woman, and everyone here is going to figure that out at some point. But when she looks at me, her eyes tell me that she already knows where I am, and that all of this is part of our journey together. When we hold hands, she transfers some of her courage to me, and I stand up a little straighter.

As I repeat my vows it begins to feel like we are stepping into a small boat together at the start of a river...at midnight. We know there will be twists and turns, rough rapids, and even some water-falls, but we can't see where they are, and once the boat is moving, we won't be able to stop it. When it is her turn to repeat her vows, I get the sense that she feels the same thing. There is no turning back now. There is too much momentum. She begins to cry, and because she is carrying everyone else in her energy, they feel what she feels, and I see women and men in the audience start wiping their own tears. When the ceremony ends, we kiss, and in that kiss, she tells me, "We are doing this, Portnoy. You and me. We got this." She is fearless. No, ferocious. I let more of her courage wash through me, and I accept her challenge. *We are doing this. Let's do this!*

The rest of the wedding day is flawless. Our family and friends. The food and the music. We follow some advice we received from our wedding officiant and stay close together as much as we can. Whatever fears we had earlier are gradually replaced with excite-ment about the adventure we are embarking on together. Just like in our early days of college, it is us against the world again, and we are ready for action.

And there is never a shortage of action...

After a beautiful honeymoon, I get straight back to working hard at Clarium. Peter has the Midas touch, and that first year the firm's returns are stellar. Anne Marie and I can hardly believe our eyes when we see the size of my bonus that December. The next year isn't quite as exciting, but then the third year the firm is firing on all cylinders again. Assets under management have grown considerably, and Peter's investment bets are right. That third year my bonus is more than all the money I've ever made from PayPal stock options or Clarium bonuses *combined*. It is a huge windfall, and it is also disorienting.

Up until now I have been fairly open with my parents about how well Anne Marie and I are doing financially. They are proud and I am proud. But as the numbers grow, I find it tougher to share the good news with them. They worked hard their whole lives and had never been rewarded this way financially. Guilt sets in. Then my parents start to make jokes about me buying things for them, and somehow the jokes don't seem funny to me.

At one point, my father suggests that a son who has done as well as I have would offer to repay the student loans his father is still carrying. It feels like an awkward suggestion. *Why can't you just be happy for me, Dad? Why are you making this about you?* But I'm confused by the feelings. Anne Marie and I talk about it, but neither of us has been in a situation like this before and we don't have elders who can guide us. We realize we'll have to figure this out ourselves. Eventually I send my dad a check in an effort to assuage some of my guilt.

As Peter's wealth and celebrity grow, so does the complexity of my life at work. We start building the foundations of a family office for him to keep things organized, an effort I help lead. We launch the Founders Fund to formalize his venture capital investments, and I become the first CFO of that fund. Clarium's assets and employee count continue to scale.

I wake up one day and realize I have three jobs, none of which I'm particularly qualified for, and the requirements for each of them is escalating quickly. I am learning on the job, and if I'm honest about it, I am drowning. But I'm not honest about it. I race to try to keep pace. By the end of that third year at Clarium, I am routinely working nights and weekends. Even if I'm not at the office I am tied to my phone or buried in my laptop. But it isn't enough. I continue falling behind.

And gradually, predictably, my constant working starts to take its toll on my marriage. After three years of being on-call 24/7 I am more like a ghost in our relationship than a life partner. Anne Marie and I go to Healdsburg two or three weekends a month to be with her family, but I spend most of my time there at a nearby coffee shop working all day. Eventually it seems pointless for me to even go, so I just stay in the city and work while she goes. I justify the sacrifice by pointing to graphs of our climbing net worth, but we both know something isn't right.

One Saturday morning I wake up to the sounds of fog horns on the Golden Gate Bridge. Anne Marie is in Healdsburg, and I'm planning to go to the office today, as usual. As I lay in bed staring at the ceiling, a new feeling starts to trickle into my body: failure. I am confused by its arrival. *Failure? Here? Me?* This is not a feeling I am used to or expecting to find, but once it arrives I feel it all around me. I am failing at work. And now I am failing Anne Marie too.

But I have become a one-trick pony by now. If an uncomfortable feeling enters my space, I bury it, or run away from it, or both. It's a technique I learned when I was a kid, and so far, it has served me pretty well. I mean look at my life. It's great, right? Isn't it? At least it felt great until this morning. Suddenly I'm not sure it's so great anymore. Then I hear a voice inside. *You don't have time for this. Stop feeling sorry for yourself. You want to be a rich, successful man, then man up and get to the office.* I push the feelings aside and dutifully follow instructions.

Unfortunately, it soon becomes apparent that no amount of effort at work can compensate for my lack of experience. Clarium is growing too fast, and now the rest of the team knows I'm falling behind too. Peter takes the necessary step of promoting one of the firm's top traders to Chief Operating Officer and demotes me to a smaller role. He knows it's hard for me to hear and he assures me that he and the team value my contributions. To avoid my feelings of failure I say something hot-headed, but he lets it go. We both know this is the right decision.

The experience takes a toll on me emotionally, though, and I take a step back and think more critically about my life. I had been so caught up in the whirlwind of "success" that I was only staring at my feet. Now I start to look up, to zoom out and see my life from a larger vantage point. No longer tethered to my screen, I start to ask myself: *Is this really the job I want? Do I really want to be estranged from Anne Marie?*

The answer to both questions is a resounding, *No.*

* * *

A FEW MONTHS LATER, IN the spring of 2007, Anne Marie and I are sitting at the small IKEA table in our kitchen, sipping some wine after dinner. We've been admiring the accent wall we just painted in our apartment. The color is Mexico City Yellow, and it makes us feel so worldly. I've been working less the last few months and we've been together more, and this moment feels warm and right.

"I want to travel more," she says, staring at the yellow wall.

"Me too," I answer, watching her. We are quiet for a minute while the thought fills the room.

Eventually I ask, "Where would you want to go?"

"Anywhere," she says softly. There is a longing in her voice. "Everywhere," she adds.

"Everywhere?"

She turns toward me and looks me in the eye. "Yeah. I want to go *everywhere*."

"Oh, wow...Like travel around the world?"

"Yes! Wouldn't that be awesome?" I hear excitement rising in her voice, but already I am nervous about leaving the safety blanket of my work.

"For how long?"

"I don't know," she says casually. "A year?"

My eyes pop out and I almost spit out my wine. "A year?!"

"Yeah." She laughs and finishes her wine, then adds, "Where are your balls, Portnoy?"

I swallow hard. I have never been as brave as Anne Marie, and we both know it.

"How about six months?" I offer.

"That could work," she says, nodding slowly.

And with that, our decision is made. We are going to travel around the world for six months. It feels insane, but it also feels like something we are doing together, and we have missed doing things together. Over the next few months, we make a budget, figure out the locations, and line up our plane tickets. I tell Peter I want to leave Clarium, and he helps me land a role as the first Chief Financial Officer at one of his most promising portfolio companies, Palantir Technologies. They aren't looking for a head of finance right now, so the CEO, Alex Karp, suggests I start in eight months, which aligns perfectly with the trip Anne Marie and I have planned.

She gets the green light to take time off from her job too, and before we know it we are sitting on a plane heading west over the Pacific Ocean, filled with anticipation for the adventure ahead of us. It feels right. We are together, floating through the world again.

* * *

IT IS A SUNNY SUMMER morning one year later and I'm at the Palantir Technologies office in Palo Alto, California. I drove down from San Francisco early this morning to put the finishing touches on a financial model that I'll be reviewing with Alex later today. My office is spartan—just a desk, a chair, and a computer—but that's fine with me. There has been so much to do since I got here in January that I haven't had time to worry about anything else.

After I double check the numbers, I lean back in my chair and admire my work. Building models like this for fast-growing Silicon Valley startup companies has become one of my signature skills. I first learned how to do it from Roelof, my manager at PayPal, and I've done it a million times since. I am proud of my work, and confident in my abilities. Any ideas that I might be failing in my work are a distant memory.

Anne Marie and I returned from our round-the-world trip last December refreshed, reconnected, and ready to jump back into our careers. Our trip was incredible. A stroke of genius on her part. What sounded like a crazy idea when she first voiced it turned out to be exactly what we needed for ourselves and for our relationship. I wasn't failing at my marriage anymore either. Another boost of pride.

And as if to fan the flames, Palantir as a company is blowing up, in a good way. Late last year the company closed a financing at a much higher value than the prior round. Facebook is already a darling of Silicon Valley, and when word gets out about the financing, Palantir is increasingly viewed as Peter Thiel's "next big thing." Many years ago, Anne Marie and I invested a sizeable chunk of my Clarium bonus money into Palantir, and the latest valuation made us big money on paper. But it isn't just the money. Almost overnight, it feels like being an employee at Palantir is like being a mini celebrity in the Silicon Valley microculture. More pride sets in, and soon I notice that I walk a little taller when I'm wearing my Palantir track jacket around town.

I am riding high on the wave now, and on the outside my life looks perfect. Stanford, PayPal, CFO at Palantir. Career success, financial success, amazing wife, fancy car. My friends are congratulating me. My parents are proud. I am convinced I'm doing all the right things. What could be wrong with this story?

It turns out, a lot was wrong. I never really outgrew some of my childhood habits and coping mechanisms. The dual nature that developed back in elementary school, the one where I put on a front that told the world everything was fine in my life when it wasn't, remained. As did my ability to distract myself from emotions I couldn't handle by engaging in attention- and thrill-seeking behaviors. By the time I was a working adult, I'd mastered maintaining a persona that suggested everything was wonderful in my life, while an alter ego, intent on creating chaos, came to life.

Consequently, I couldn't take my successes in stride. I didn't have a solid foundation that enabled me to do that. Instead, I had the euphoria and invincibility of fast, young wealth. The guilt of having more than my family. The isolation of not being able to talk about it with anyone. Combined, it all created a confusing cocktail of emotions, which I handled the only way I knew how: distraction and pretense.

I put on the everything-is-wonderful persona for the world to see in the light of day, while my alter ego dabbled in the darkness of night. It was a delicate balance that not even Anne Marie was aware I maintained, even though I'd been managing it for years. College was when the secrets began piling up. Eventually, they became so thick, my alter ego lived an entire separate life within them.

PART 2

SEARCHING IN THE DARK

CHAPTER 4

"Every man is a moon and has a side which he turns toward nobody: you have to slip around behind it if you want to see it."

—MARK TWAIN

NOVEMBER 1996

I AM IN MY COLLEGE BEDROOM IN BOULDER, COLORADO, in a house some friends and I are renting just north of campus. It is my third year, and I am deep in the grip of my first major-specific chemical engineering courses. The material is harder than anything I've come across yet. *No wonder those chemical engineers get paid so much. This shit is impenetrable!* I bury myself in my books to learn the new concepts.

It is dark and late by the time I finish a marathon assignment. Up until now, I've been spending late nights in the computer lab, but my father just bought me a laptop with a modem card, and now I can do my homework at my desk at home. To unwind after my homework, I surf the web, starting from my usual launch point, the Yahoo! home page. I click and follow a few interesting links, then I see something about "babes" or "bikinis" that catches my attention. A few clicks later, I'm on a site with dozens of links lined up in neat rows and columns, each the title of a different genre of porn: Blondes, Threesomes, Kinky...The choices are almost overwhelming.

Curious, I click on one, and I'm taken to another page with dozens more links, again lined up in neat rows and columns. I click one there, and the image takes a few seconds to load. Up pops a picture of a woman giving a guy a blowjob.

"Whoa," I say out loud. Quickly, I turn around and look at my bedroom door to make sure it's closed. Porn has never been part of my life before. When I was a kid, there was one time when a friend found a stash of "nudie" magazines in his parents' closet. We looked at them and laughed for a few minutes, but then we soon went back to more interesting things like soccer and skateboards. But even though I haven't been around porn, I think I know what the guy code says about it: every guy knows that every guy looks at it, but it is not okay to be *seen* looking at it. At least that's what I've picked up over the years from TV, movies, magazines, and other guys. Porn is just something guys do. Men are supposed to make money, drive sports cars, have beautiful women, and look at porn. Everyone knows that, right?

I turn back to my screen and stare in shock for a minute. Maybe it is more than a minute.

I click the back button and then click on another link.

Holy shit.

Something is happening here. A new kind of electricity courses through my body. *I shouldn't be doing this.*

I click another link. And another.

I click back twice and try a different genre.

Oh, wow.

There's a sensation in my boxers. I continue clicking links, and soon I am turned on. Slowly the room fades away. My computer is the only thing I see. Once again, just like when I was a kid watching television, I disappear into a screen.

* * *

IN THE MONTHS AND YEARS that follow, the world of online pornography unfolds before my eyes. By the time Anne Marie and I return from our round-the-world trip at the end of 2007, I am thirty-one years old and have been looking at internet porn and masturbating for eleven years. I am a daily user. Occasionally I skip a few days, but there are other times when, either because of boredom or stress, I might look at porn multiple times in a single day. I definitely consider it a habit, but it doesn't bother me. I'm an adult, and porn is just a release valve for stress, right?

As my life had progressed, with each rung up the ladder of success, expectations on me grew and pressures mounted. It started with pressure to get good grades in Colorado; pressure that compounded when I tried to continue that trend at Stanford. The pressures at PayPal were even bigger. By the time I was working at Clarium Capital, it wasn't just the confusing blend of emotions from fast/young wealth and internal isolation anymore, or even the newest pressure of wanting to be a good husband. As the firm grew, and the dollar signs grew, and I struggled to keep pace with my escalating responsibilities, the pressure I experienced from all sides was almost unbearable.

Now at Palantir, my bigger salary and bigger title means bigger expectations from my bosses and my peers. I feel increasing expectations from employees, from my parents, from Anne Marie, from myself, from society. There are so many expectations, and so much pressure to live up to what I think everyone expects from me, that I begin to lose track of who I am.

Against this backdrop, porn became my place to escape. To disappear. The women on the screen expected nothing from me. And when I was alone, in the dark with my computer, the whole world fell away. Nothing else existed. *Nobody* expected *anything* from me. It was my time to be alone. And then, in that final moment of climax, I could go numb. Numb to the world. Numb to a lifetime of confusing feelings I had been burying and running away from since I was a child. Numb to all the pressures and expectations I felt as an adult.

Gradually, it sucked me in. And, because the porn industry is so massive, and the amount of porn on the internet is essentially infinite, it was easy for me to justify: I assumed every other guy was looking at porn too. *This is normal. It's what men do. Some guys use TV as their escape, others watch porn.* But despite thinking it was normal, I never told anyone about my habit. I kept it hidden. It was my little secret.

My childhood training in how to live two parallel lives came in handy as my habit grew. I knew how to keep secrets. How to lie. When I was younger, there was my life at home, where I felt angry, helpless, and alone; and there was my life at school or with my friends, where I learned to say "Everything's great. Let's have fun!"

As an adult, there was my private time with porn, and there was the pressure and expectations of everything else. At one point, late in college, I tried to bridge the two worlds. During one of our "on" periods, I asked Anne Marie if we could watch porn together. She reluctantly agreed, but porn didn't do the same things for her that it did for me, and afterward she said she didn't want to watch it again. She also felt like I was cheating on her if I watched those women on the screen, so I told her I would stop looking at porn. It would have been more honest to say, *I guess these two sides of me can't be bridged, so one will have to stay in the shadows.*

After that I took my porn completely underground, intending to never talk to Anne Marie about it again. And as the years progressed, hiding my porn habit from Anne Marie introduced two new powerful feelings into my adult life: guilt and shame. Guilt because I was lying to Anne Marie. Shame because I knew I shouldn't be. Pressure and expectations. Guilt and shame. Altogether, they make a powerful brew.

What I didn't understand was that, for me, porn was a drug. And like any other drug, it demanded more of me the more I used it.

When I first started looking at porn in college, it was over a dial-up modem, with data transfer speeds that were very slow. Individual images were not very high quality, and they took a long time to load, so the amount of porn I could consume at any given time was limited. But as the years went by and technology improved, download speeds increased, and so did the quality and resolution of the images on my screen. Eventually websites began offering short video clips. Before long it was an unlimited supply of high-resolution, long format porn videos—complete with sound—all immediately available with a click of a button. *Boom!* Instant immersive porn. Instant powerful dopamine hits. Every day, I closed my bedroom door, got online, disappeared, and went numb. When I returned to reality, a wave of guilt and shame would hit me like a wall, and I'd struggle to hold myself together until I could disappear again.

Much later, I learn our brain receptors are sensitive; they are not built for this kind of sustained stimulation. Correction, *overstimulation.* As the years passed, my brain did what brains do: it became desensitized to the chemicals released with porn and climax. After a while, still images just didn't have the same effect on me anymore. When short video clips arrived, they weren't just a nice new option, I *needed* them to get the same rush I had previously felt from the pictures. Then short video clips just weren't cutting it; I *needed* long-format videos. Unfortunately, the day eventually arrived when even high-resolution videos just weren't enough. I needed something stronger.

* * *

IT IS A WARM SUMMER night in 2002. PayPal went public a few months ago and the stock price is climbing. My newfound wealth is still all on paper, but the post IPO lockup period will expire soon, and I'll be able to start selling some of my shares. I'm feeling good. I'm feeling *really* good.

The bright lights of the airport pass me on the right as I make my way up 101 from Mountain View to San Francisco. My pickup truck isn't fancy, but it is practical, and it gets the job done. The stereo is off because I'm too amped up for music right now, and my mind is spinning faster and faster as I approach the city. *What is she going to look like? What is going to happen? Is it safe for me to be going to a strange woman's apartment alone?*

Anne Marie flashes through my mind, but I quickly bury the image. She has been in Los Angeles the last six months and what she doesn't know won't hurt her. I notice how cold and callous it feels when I think that, and then I quickly bury that feeling too. *I'm on a mission. I deserve this. Nothing is going to stop me.*

Ever since Anne Marie left for Los Angeles I have been alone, a lot. I'd been working so many hours for so long by now that I've lost touch with most of my friends. The process of taking PayPal public was brutally time-consuming. This was before the days of ubiquitous connectivity and VPNs, so most of the work had to be done in the office. Often, I left work so late at night that I had just enough time to sleep a few hours, take a shower, and head back to the office early the next day. But after the IPO, I suddenly went back to having a more reasonable workload. I vividly recall leaving the office some days at a normal hour and wondering what the hell to do with myself.

I started playing pickup soccer in the evenings. I bought myself a remote-control car to tinker with, a hobby I had enjoyed as a kid. After dinner, I'd watch a movie or update my personal finances spreadsheet or read. Inevitably I'd wind up in front of my computer, looking at porn before I went to bed, but that was getting boring.

At some point I realized the lease on my apartment would end soon, and that prompted me to go on Craigslist one night to start looking for a new place. I hit the home page and saw a link I'd never noticed before called "Casual Encounters." It sounded interesting. I had to check it out.

After reading a few listings, I quickly learned that Casual Encounters was a place where people placed ads for hookups, with many posts offering "no strings attached." My pulse quickened as I scanned the screen. This was a rush I'd never felt before.

And now I'm feeling it again as I park my truck in an unfamiliar neighborhood and walk toward a stranger's door. I ring the bell, and she answers quickly. "Hi!" She's bright and inviting. "Come on in."

She and her place are very bohemian. Her home is small and smoky, filled with art and texture. Her loose-fitting outfit flows around her as she crosses the room and passes a table covered with pictures and magazine clippings. All of a sudden, my life of tech companies and finance feels sterile—one dimensional, 2D at best. I feel very out of place, and it takes me time to get my bearings.

"Have a seat." She points to the couch. "Mind if I open some wine?"

She seems very prepared for this. Much more prepared than I am. I glance at the door and think I can still bail out, but something stops me.

"Wine sounds great to me."

She retrieves a bottle and opens it while I get situated on the couch.

"So how was your day?" she asks as she hands me my glass. She sits at the opposite end of the couch, which I then realize is the only piece of furniture in her tiny living room.

Our conversation was awkward at the start, but with time and some wine the tension eases, and things start to flow more naturally. After a while she reveals that she doesn't *really* just want a hookup, she's an aspiring artist looking for a guy who will pay her rent so she can focus on her art. In exchange, he can visit her a few times a week for "fun."

I tell her that, unfortunately, I can't afford to be her wealthy patron, and as soon as this comes to light, I sense that she starts to lose interest in me. I'm okay with that, though, because at some point while we were talking and getting to know each other, I realized that I didn't really care about her. I drove up here to have sex, and if that's not happening, even I'm starting to wonder what I'm doing here. For a moment, my mind zooms out and sees us from a distance, where we look like two kids pretending to be grown-ups, assuming that this is what grown-ups do.

We continue talking and drinking wine for a while and then oddly, just as I'm getting ready to leave, she decides that we should go to her bedroom since "...I had driven all the way to the city for this." She dims the lights, and we make our way to her room. The experience is odd and surreal. Maybe it's because we both assume we will never see each other again. Maybe it's because my mind is racing back and forth between *I can't believe this is happening* and *What the fuck am I doing here?*

In hindsight, the most exhilarating thing about that first hookup was not the sex, it was the entire experience *leading up to* the sex. The anticipation during our email exchanges and on my drive to the city. The danger of visiting a strange woman's apartment without having told anyone where I was going. The uncertainty of whether or not we would actually have sex. All of it added up to something much larger than the sexual act itself. At the time I didn't have the awareness to understand why I felt such a rush; all I knew was that it was exhilarating. So much so that, as I drove out of the city heading toward home, I vowed to double down on my Craigslist efforts. The real-life experience was so much more intense than masturbating to online porn. I needed more.

A month later I have a second encounter. This time I take things up a notch and post my own listing on Craigslist. A few women reply, and I arrange to meet one at a casual restaurant near my apartment, so we can get to know each other over a beer. The days and hours leading up to our meeting are filled with that same luscious yet anxious anticipation, but after the experience, I do not feel exhilarated. I feel like shit.

The following week, I go through the motions at work, but my mind is somewhere else. I push food around on my plate at mealtimes, unable to actually eat. I love Anne Marie, and I miss her. Not telling her about porn was one thing, but cheating was an entirely different violation of trust. I tell myself I won't do it again. And I don't. For a while.

* * *

ALMOST EXACTLY ONE YEAR LATER, only months before our wedding, I find myself alone at my computer one night, browsing listings on Craigslist again. Anne Marie and I live together in San Francisco now. She has already gone to bed, and I'm staying up late to finish some work. Of course, after I finish my work, I look at porn. And for some reason, on this night, I am drawn back to Craigslist.

Just like before, I have two different encounters over the course of a few months. After the second one I feel sick. More importantly, I feel like I'm losing control of myself. For the first time I share what I've done with my best friend, which, looking back, I realize was a cry for help. I vow, like last time, to never do it again. When am I going to learn?

Two years later, I find myself laying in bed one night, staring at the ceiling. Soft light from the San Francisco skyline trickles through the miniblinds in our bedroom window. Anne Marie is to my left, curled in a fetal position facing away from me. It is her typical sleeping pose. We just got in bed and said our goodnights a few minutes ago, and the room still smells like the oil she puts on after her nighttime shower. I don't know what the scent is. All I know is that she smells delicious.

She can't be asleep already. I roll toward her and put my hand on her shoulder. She doesn't move. I gently rub her arm.

"J." Her voice is low. The sound is somewhere between a question and a growl. In one syllable she has communicated two complete sentences: "Why are you touching me?" and "Goodnight, I'm going to sleep now."

Undeterred, I lean closer to kiss the back of her neck.

Her body seems to leap off the bed as she turns around. She's so quick, she startles me.

"Seriously, J?!" she pleads, exasperated.

I act befuddled, feign amusement. "Whaaaat? Whaaaat?" I throw my hands up and try to sound innocent, realizing that, in this moment, I sound like a kid who just got caught with his hand in the cookie jar.

"I'm tired." She fluffs her pillow. "It's too late for that."

And with that, the conversation is over.

I roll onto my back and stare at the ceiling again. *Too late? So I should have tried at dinner time? She would have said that was a weird time. I can't win!*

After two years of marriage, it has become apparent that Anne Marie and I have very different expectations for the amount of sex we should have in our relationship. Put simply, I want it more frequently than she does. She can go weeks and months without. It just isn't important to her. But it is important to me.

We are falling into a routine that I later learn traps a lot of couples: I feel like I need sex to feel close to her; she needs to feel close to me before she's interested in sex. Gradually, it becomes an unbreakable cycle for both of us. I am always on-call and working so much that she definitely doesn't feel close to me. The more I ask for sex, the more it turns her off, and as she continues to reject my advances, I increasingly feel rejected. Rejection hurts, so to avoid that feeling I bury myself in my work. Or I watch more porn. More distance, more rejection. Lather, rinse, repeat.

I never consider that my secrets and lies could be contributing to any distance that has developed between us. Or that after a decade of porn and a half dozen hookups, sex is more like a means to an end for me. Or that Anne Marie's body instinctively, and accurately, knows not to trust me. These concepts seem so obvious to me now, but they were far too advanced for me back then. As far as I was concerned, Anne Marie just didn't want to have sex with me, and gradually I started to resent her for it.

Maybe because of that, the third time I go back to Craigslist for a Casual Encounter, I do so with a vengeance. Aside from porn, I have been faithful since our wedding. Now, I feel completely justified in what I'm doing; there is no guilt to hold me back. *This is just what men do. They take charge, and they go after what they want. I'm a successful man and I want sex—no, I* deserve *sex—and so I'm justified in getting it through whatever means necessary.*

After a week of scanning listings again, I discover something new: now there are escorts on Craigslist. *This* is a whole new world. So instead of browsing endless listings and exchanging tons of emails, I can just pay a woman to spend time with me? *Well, that seems so much better, right?*

The world of online escorts blows my mind. The listings on Craigslist are just the tip of the iceberg. I find a dozen free listing websites where I can browse profiles. When I find one I like, I click through to her website. There I see pages of photos and get detailed information about how the process will work, how much it will cost, what is (or is not) allowed, etc. It is all there, out in the open. The more expensive escorts will even arrange a hotel room to meet in, which means I don't even have to worry about logistics.

And this is how my philandering goes to the next level: with escorts. For the next year and a half, up until the point when Anne Marie and I leave for our round-the-world trip, I am stuck in a new, vicious cycle. I meet an escort, then I feel horrible about what I've done, and I vow to never do it again. Then three or four months later I start resenting Anne Marie again for our lack of intimacy, I forget how bad I felt after cheating the last time, and

I set up another meeting. Again, I feel terrible, and again I vow never to do it again.

The cycle starts to eat away at me, and eventually the tone of my confessions to my best friend escalate to, "Man, I have a problem." I know what I'm doing is wrong, but when the urges wash over me, I am powerless to stop them. I have all kinds of justifications: I'm in a sexless marriage; I *deserve* this; monogamy isn't biologically natural. Now that I have cheated so many times without getting caught, there was the newest justification: Anne Marie would never know, so it wasn't a big deal.

The justifications were all bullshit. I was spinning out of control, and deep down, I knew it.

When Anne Marie suggested that we take our trip around the world, it was a blessing and a relief. I told myself that I would reset on that trip, and never cheat again. I'd be away from San Francisco and the stresses and pressures of work. And I wouldn't have to pass by places where I'd had secret meetings, which had increasingly grown to haunt me as I moved around the city. *Yes! Let's get out of here. I need to get out of here.*

Our trip around the world really did reset things for us. We came back refreshed and reconnected, and I felt like my old life was behind me. I was starting from a clean slate. I even had a new job to focus on at Palantir. But I had done nothing to address the fundamental issues that had driven me into the dark in the past. Just below the surface, my alter ego was a ticking timebomb. All I needed was the right trigger, and in October of that year, she arrived.

CHAPTER 5

"...for a man needs only to be turned round once with his eyes shut in this world to be lost..."

—HENRY DAVID THOREAU, *Walden*

OCTOBER 2008

I AM LYING ON THE BEACH IN HAWAII. THE EVENING SUN is low enough that I don't need an umbrella to protect me from the heat, and I'm enjoying the feeling of the warmth on my skin. The repetition of the waves lulls me into a trance, and I stare out over the horizon, just peripherally aware of the kids playing in the surf. We only landed in Hawaii a few hours ago, but already I'm so relaxed that I feel like we've been here for days. It is a perfect setting for us to celebrate our five-year anniversary.

Anne Marie comes back from the room, but she doesn't lay back down on her towel. Instead, she plops down on her knees facing me, with a look on her face that says she knows something and can't wait to tell me.

"What's up?" I ask.

"We're pregnant!" She blurts it out excitedly.

"Seriously?! Oh my god!"

We give each other a long hug, then she curls up next to me, and we watch the sunset together, eagerly cataloging the changes that are about to take place for us.

"I'll have to find a doctor when we get back," she says.

"Yeah, and we'll have to make space in the apartment."

"Wow," she sighs. "A baby. We're going to have a baby."

* * *

TWO MONTHS LATER, WE ARE shopping for a new home. Our small apartment is not a good place to welcome a newborn. The building is falling into disrepair, and we need more space. We find a condo that seems to offer what we need, close on it in early January, and quickly move in.

I am ecstatic about the idea of welcoming a baby into our lives, and for the first few weeks I walk on clouds. However, after the initial rosy flush of excitement, the dawning of my new realities sends me into a tailspin.

I am going to be a father, which means I'll have a family to support; the financial pressures ratchet up immediately. Buying a condo means coming up with a down payment and taking out a big mortgage. We'll have to start saving for college soon. If we stay in the city, which we really want to do, it probably means private schools. Each new item is accompanied by the sound of a cash register as I do the mental accounting. *Cha-ching. Cha-ching. Cha-ching.* We have done well financially, but anyone living in San Francisco knows that even a couple million dollars doesn't feel like a lot when measured against the cost of living here. My internal response is simple: *I'll just work harder.*

But beyond the financial pressure, there is a deeper fear. I know what my shortcomings are. I know where I have already fallen short at being a husband. Inside, I am terrified about being a father. *I'm not ready. I'm just not ready.* So I go back to my usual playbook. I return to the places where I am most comfortable. I disappear into my work during the daytime and evenings, and I disappear into porn at night. Eventually, I disappear on Anne Marie.

I start skipping the pregnancy doctor appointments. "I have an important meeting at work," I say. "Do you mind going alone?"

"Sure, it's fine," she always says. "I can go by myself." We both know she doesn't mean it, but I don't let that stop me.

Predictably, our growing emotional distance means the loss of intimacy in our relationship again, although this time it isn't just Anne Marie feeling this way. I, too, have lost interest in marital sex, preferring the simplicity of late-night pornography to the emotional complexity of true intimate connection.

Only four months after finding out we are pregnant, we once again find ourselves in a downward spiral. Like most young couples, we try to figure things out for ourselves, which in hindsight seems crazy. If only we had sought out guidance, maybe someone could have helped steer us through the tangled web of emotions we were both feeling. But we didn't do that. Instead, it is just the two of us, once again alone in our little boat, rushing down the river without any guiding lights. We don't have any tools to help us deal with what we are experiencing. All we know is that something isn't right. We both start resenting each other, and in this precious time when we should be coming closer together, we begin drifting further and further apart.

My evening work sessions at home gradually morph into me choosing to stay at the office and work late from there. Once every week or two, I work so late and need to be back so early the next day, that I just stay at a hotel near the office instead of making the two-hour roundtrip drive. Our due date is in May; the next few months will be my final big push at work to wrap up some major projects before I take time off after the baby arrives.

"You sure you're okay with me staying down here tonight?" I ask Anne Marie.

Once again, she says, "Sure, that's fine." Once again, we both know she is lying. And once again, I do not let that stop me.

Sometime in February, a networking dinner turns into drinks after dinner, which turns into me inviting one of the women I've met back to my hotel room. We leave the bar separately so we won't be suspicious. I stop at a convenience store to buy condoms on my way to the hotel. *Just in case.* She arrives at my hotel about fifteen minutes after me, and those fifteen minutes feel like hours. The anticipation is electric. This isn't a Craigslist hookup, or a transaction with an escort. No, this is something entirely new and different.

My heart pounds everywhere in my body as I read her text message.

I'm here. What room are you in?

A few minutes later, she knocks on the door; letting her in, I sense she is feeling the same things I am: some powerful combination of excitement and fear. Excitement for what is about to happen, fear because we are both terrified of anyone finding out.

I begin seeing this woman on a regular basis. As the weeks pass, my alter ego takes over and I lose all sense of direction. I have no bearing anymore. No compass. I move through life like an animal. I have instincts and reactions, but no conscious thought. Periodically,

I wake up and immediately feel ashamed of myself. I don't try to justify my behavior—I can't. I don't even tell my best friend what is happening; I'm too embarrassed. The shame is so intense that I numb out completely. I stop caring about anything anymore.

Before this new phase, I was a guy trying to live in the light while his shadow side dabbled in the dark. Now the tables have turned. I am totally in the dark now, and Anne Marie, my lighthouse, is fading further and further away. In the dark there are no expectations. No work. No wife. No baby on the way. In the dark, my shadow-self rules while the other me can abandon all responsibility and go to sleep. In the dark I can disappear. In the dark I can go numb.

The affair continues for almost four months, ending a few weeks before our baby is expected to arrive. By then, Anne Marie and I are like two ships passing in the night. What should be a time of profound closeness for us is exactly the opposite. We cannot be further apart. I haven't been present for most of her journey through pregnancy. When we go to a birthing class the month before our due date, I feel like a fish out of water, and I can't understand how all the other dads seem so much more knowledgeable about what is about to happen than I am.

But babies don't wait until you are ready. Babies don't wait until your relationship is in the exact right place. Babies arrive on their schedule, not yours. Our baby was no different.

* * *

I EXIT A TEAM MEETING at work and settle back into my desk to check emails. It is just after noon on a Wednesday, and the office is bustling. I get a text message from Anne Marie.

Having contractions…timing them…call when you can.

My heart skips a beat. *It's time.*

In a rush, I gather my things, knowing I won't be back in the office for several weeks. My team and I are prepared, so there aren't any last-minute details to iron out. My assistant squeals "Go go go!" as I run out the door. I jump in my car and make my way up Highway 101 like a Formula 1 driver.

At home, Anne Marie is lying on our bed. My mom sits near her, using a stopwatch to keep track of the contractions. My eyes quickly meet Anne Marie's, and she gives me a look and a nod that says, "Yes, it's time." I grab our pre-packed hospital bags and load them in the car while Anne Marie's parents help her down our apartment stairs. The drive to the hospital is short, and everyone knows what to do when we get there. Several hours later, Maya Cochran Portnoy enters the world, a perfect baby girl. Anne Marie and I both fall in love with her immediately.

There are cultures who believe that the spirit of a child chooses its parents before it is born into a physical body. I now believe this too. When Maya entered our family, Anne Marie and I were in a very fragile space. The long-term effects of our childhood wounds, which had never been identified, much less addressed, were beginning to show themselves. The feelings of isolation, of "not fitting in," that I'd felt as a child, mixed with my tendency to bury or avoid confusing feelings, had pushed me to dissociate from my most intimate relationships. In parallel, a lifetime of gender stereotypes led me to seek out external validation and social acceptance through money, cars, and women. I was not in a healthy place, and Anne Marie was going through her own challenges as well.

We had a sense that something wasn't right in our relationship, but we didn't know how to identify what it was. We needed help, but we didn't know how to ask for it, or whom to ask. Fortunately for us, Maya knew how to help us. Unfortunately for Maya, I would be a slow student.

About ten days after Maya's birth, Anne Marie is napping in our bedroom with Maya napping beside her in her bouncer. The two of them are inseparable. Anne Marie's instincts have kicked in, and she is a perfect mother with a singular purpose: nurture the baby. As I watch her with Maya, I am struck by how responsible she is. In addition to embracing her maternal instinct, she has read a stack of books about pregnancy and early childcare. She's never been a mother before, but she seems to know exactly what to do in every circumstance. I am simultaneously awestruck by her level of preparation and embarrassed by my lack of it.

Grandparents swarm everywhere. One cooks. One cleans. One does laundry. A fourth just came back from the grocery store with more supplies. Our condo isn't a condo anymore; it is a hive. The workers remain busy taking care of every detail so the queen can nurture the young.

I'm on the couch reading a book about how to be a good father. Glancing up to take in the scene, I realize how disconnected I am from my life at home; I am merely a spectator here now. Anne Marie had nine months with a baby growing inside her as a constant reminder of what was on the horizon. Nine months to prepare herself, her growing body gradually forcing her to slow down and be ready for this moment. I, on the other hand, was completely absent, physically and emotionally. As I watch the activity, I begin to wonder what my place is here. *What am I supposed to be doing? When will my instincts kick in?*

I feel dizzy and disoriented—being on paternity leave is like being in detox, and I have withdrawal symptoms. I haven't just been absent in my marriage, I've been spinning like a top, rotating quickly from one focus to another so I didn't have to connect with anything, or anyone. The world remained gray that way. I didn't have to be present. This forced domesticity took all that away. With no work, no affair, and no privacy in our home (so no porn), the spinning slowed. Soon it would stop, and I'd crash into...what?

Over the next few days, it slowed to the point where it became unbearable. The blurry grayness was gradually replaced by vibrant colors and sharper images. I began to notice things I hadn't noticed before. The leaves on the Magnolia tree outside our front window. I can see each one now. I hear birds chirping. I instantly realize that they have always been there, but I hadn't heard them until now. Anne Marie smiles and kisses Maya's cheeks, and the grandparents ooh and aah. The world is coming alive all around me, but it's too much. It's too bright. It's too loud. I'm not programmed to handle such a vivid life. I become antsy, fidgety. After a few more days, I feel agitated. My skin is itchy, just like when I was a kid. *I have to get out of here.*

"I have to go to the office today to pick up some papers," I announce one morning. "I'll be back in a few hours."

The family waves me off, and I depart. As soon as the door of our condo closes behind me, the colors start to fade again. The darkness welcomes me back with open arms. My shoulders drop, my jaw unclenches. I am home.

I do not go to the office to pick up papers. I go to a hotel, and an escort I'd met years earlier greets me at the door to her room. I walk inside, and I disappear.

* * *

DRIVING HOME FROM THE HOTEL that afternoon, I think about what it will be like to go back into our condo with Anne Marie and Maya and our parents. I expect to feel ashamed, but I'm not. A new feeling overtakes me that I haven't felt before: disgust. I am disgusted with myself. I turn onto our street, acknowledging to myself that I'd hit a new low. It was, indeed, a new low. It was disgusting. *I* was disgusting. I walk back into the condo, into the vibrant world of real life, and I lie about my visit to the office. As the words come out of my mouth, I sense a small part of myself die. Like I have snuffed out the last glimmers of light inside myself.

I can't look any of them in the eye, so I tell everyone I'm tired and go straight to our bedroom. I shower to try to clean the darkness off myself. As I dry off, I catch a glimpse of myself in the mirror and I pause. I don't even recognize the guy I see looking back at me. He looks lost. He looks confused. When I look into his eyes, he does not look like a man who is ready to be either a husband or a father. He looks like a boy. A scared boy. I quickly look away, too ashamed of what I see.

I climb in bed, bundle myself in the thick comforter, and curl up in a fetal position. The stillness of the room is a huge weight pressing me into the bed. My body shivers. I am alone. I am scared. I hate myself. I have already failed as a husband, and now, only a few weeks in, I am failing as a father.

Why is this happening to me? I thought I was doing every-thing right. I got good grades. I got good jobs. I made good money. A wife. A car. A nice house. Now a baby. I did everything I was supposed to do. Even the cheating felt like something that was expected of me. I've watched countless TV shows and movies where boyfriends or husbands cheated. I've been told countless times that "Men are dogs." And what about all the politicians and other men in high profile positions who were exposed in the

media because they were cheating, or predators, or both? I was just doing what I thought was expected of me as a man.
Something has to change. *I can't keep living like this.*

* * *

IT IS A SUNNY WEEKDAY in late November, and we are heading north on 101 to spend Thanksgiving with our families. Anne Marie is driving, and we can hear the soft sounds of Maya snoozing in her car seat behind us. I'm staring out the window, zoning as I watch the beautiful fall colors pass by.

Over the past five months, I've re-examined all the playbooks I felt society had ever handed me. I am a diligent student, but not because I'm trying to follow through on what the playbooks suggest. Instead, I'm trying to find the flaws. As I get more critical about my own programming, I start to notice things about my peers I hadn't noticed before. For starters, a bunch of them are getting divorced. There are various reasons, and in at least one case the cause is infidelity. On the outside, these men look like they have everything, but I start to wonder if they are as miserable on the inside as I am. *Maybe they have secrets too.*

I turn to look at Anne Marie. I miss her. I have been faithful since the encounter just after Maya was born, but the demands of my job are relentless, and I still disappear into my work more than I am present with her and Maya. The company is growing so fast, there is just no getting around the workload, and she and I are as distant as we've ever been. While I'm consumed by my work, she builds a relationship and a life with Maya. In the weeks after Maya was born, I felt like a spectator. Now when I am home, I feel like an interloper. I barely belong there. They have their schedule, and their stroller walks around the neighborhood, and I'm just this guy who enters and exists at various times. Somewhere I know that this is not what I want for myself. I don't want to end up like the peers I'm watching get divorced. It is becoming clear that I need to make a decision soon: my work, or my family.

"I'm going to quit my job," I blurt out.

Anne Marie's eyes open wide. "What?" she asks.

"Palantir. I'm going to quit next week."

"Are you sure?" she asks.

"Yes, I'm sure. I want to be with you and Maya."

"Wow." She doesn't look over at me.

I wait for her to be excited, but it doesn't happen. I turn and look out the windshield. *That's weird. My work. My career. The title. The money. These are how I've defined myself for years. Offering to give them up is the greatest peace offering I can make, and this is her reaction?*

I turn and stare out my window again and it dawns on me that I haven't actually been connecting *all* of the dots. When I rewind the film, I realize Anne Marie stopped complaining about my work schedule a long time ago. I haven't felt any resentment from her about how much I've been at the office. I thought she had just gotten used to it, but now I realize that's not what happened at all. She stopped caring.

Shit. This is worse than I thought.

Anne Marie's ambivalence to my announcement scares the shit out of me and lights a fire under my ass. Very quickly, saving my marriage becomes the only priority in my life.

The following week I tell my boss, Alex, about my decision. He is not surprised. I have been open with him about my struggles to balance work and family the last few months, but he didn't need me to tell him. He is a brilliant man and a keen observer; I knew he could sense things weren't right in my life on a deeper level. He is gracious and understanding, and we agree that I will wrap things up and transition out by the end of the year.

* * *

STEP ONE WAS COMPLETE, BUT if I am going to start repairing things with Anne Marie—or just repairing my own life—I need to do more, and I am going to need help. A week later, I find myself sitting on a couch in a nondescript building in Pacific Heights talking to a marriage therapist. He is a calm, thoughtful guy, and I feel confident he is going to help me.

My last day at work is in early January. Soon after, I am on a plane to Colorado with Anne Marie and Maya for our first family vacation. Anne Marie's parents offered to meet us there so they could watch Maya and give us some alone time together. It is a good trip, and Anne Marie and I have fun skiing together, but it is clear we are struggling to connect, and the reconstruction process is going to take time. I tell her about my conversations with my therapist, and she agrees to join me for a session when we return home.

The day of the session arrives. Anne Marie sits in her chair, stone-faced, as the therapist and I share some of the things we've talked about in the preceding weeks. She doesn't say a word for most of the hour. When she finally decides to participate, it is with a question, razor sharp in its conciseness.

"Is the goal of therapy always to keep the couple together?" she asks. Completely in her style, she uses just a few words to communicate so much.

The therapist diplomatically answers while I stare at her in disbelief. I had completely misjudged the scale of the chasm that had opened between us. I suddenly realize that my goal to save our marriage is not going to be as easy as completing some project at work. *Maybe I have waited too long. Maybe it is already too late.*

CHAPTER 6

"Blessed are those brave enough to make things awkward,
for they wake us up and move us forward."

—GLENNON DOYLE, *Untamed*

MAY 2010

IT'S 2:13 IN THE MORNING ACCORDING TO MY PHONE,
and I've just been woken by a strange mechanical sound. It's pitch
black in the bedroom. I roll to my left and stretch my arm out,
but Anne Marie's side of the bed is empty. My eyes adjust to the
dark and I see a sliver of light under the bathroom door. My brain
comes online, and I realize the noise is Anne Marie's breast pump.
She had gone to a barbecue yesterday and must have stayed out
late with her friends afterward. I bury my head under my pillow
to block out the noise and quickly fall back to sleep. The last few
months have been incredible, and exhausting.

I've been diligent with attending therapy, but I haven't told my
therapist about the porn or philandering. We've mostly focused
on my relationship with Anne Marie and my fears of fatherhood,

and we've dabbled around my childhood. Though the therapy is slow going, a slog really, it must be helping somehow: I haven't cheated in a year and I'm gradually looking at porn less often. I'm making progress.

I'm also spending a lot more time with Maya now, and she is teaching me how to live in the light. I take her swimming at the YMCA, to music classes, and on stroller walks around the neighborhood. Even the smallest accomplishments, like packing her lunch and diaper bag for an outing, are huge sources of pride for me. *I can do this. I can help care for this child too. I can be a dad.*

The swim lessons are the highlight of my week. There I am, holding her head above the water while we bob around in circles singing the "Motorboat, Motorboat" song. I gently blow in her face as the instructor has taught us, so she will close her eyes and hold her breath when I dunk her. When she surfaces, we laugh and giggle together, and every minute I'm with her I can feel myself getting further from the dark.

The only place where it doesn't feel like I'm making progress is with Anne Marie. She began seeing her own therapist too, so I try to be patient. I know the full extent of damage I inflicted on our relationship over the years, and I assume it's going to take time to heal. It feels like spending time together would help the healing, but since I stopped working, we really haven't spent much time together at all. Anne Marie goes out with her friends a lot, and a few weeks ago she bailed out of joining me and Maya on a trip to visit my family on the East Coast because she needed some time for herself.

At first it all makes sense to me. I was absent for most of the pregnancy and birth, and Anne Marie had carried a heavy burden. She needs time to blow off steam and reconnect with herself and her friends. I get it. But Anne Marie hasn't gone back to work yet, and after a few months I start wondering how her friends can function at their jobs when they are all out drinking so often. I bring it up with her one night after she gets home late, but I get an icy response.

"You disappeared on me, and now you come back and I'm just supposed to drop everything for you?"

I have no good answer. She is right, and she doesn't even know half of what I've done. I don't feel like I have any moral foundation to stand on, so I let it go. But after a few more months, I just can't help feeling like something isn't right.

The morning after the barbecue, while Anne Marie is out at a yoga class, I put Maya down for her nap. When I return to our bedroom, I notice Anne Marie's bag by the foot of the bed. Curiosity takes over, and I sift through the contents. *That's funny. Why did she need a bathing suit and change of clothes to go to an afternoon barbecue in the park?*

Curiosity turns into suspicion. Where was she really going all those times when she left? Who were all the friends? I mull on that a few minutes before it occurs to me that I can check our phone bill to see who she was calling and texting.

I open my laptop at the kitchen table and log into our cell phone account. There are dozens of texts and calls to and from her number at all hours of the day and night. Scanning the list, my eyes zero in on a number that clearly shows up more than the rest, including up until two o'clock this morning. *Who is that?* I enter the number into a search on Google but no match comes up. Then I search my own contact list to see if I know the person. Sure enough, there is a match.

I crumble forward so fast my head almost hits the table. *Oh my god. She's having an affair.*

* * *

IT'S THE NEXT DAY, AND although I'm suspicious, I don't confront Anne Marie right away. I'm not 100 percent sure what's happening, and really, my mind reels so much that nothing makes sense. *Is she really having an affair? If she is, does this mean we get divorced? What about all the things I've done? Maybe we just aren't meant to be together anymore.*

I need time away from her to think. Voicing my concerns about her going out hadn't really gotten me anywhere, so I take things up a notch. When she gets back from her yoga class, I tell her that coming home at two o'clock in the morning was it for me.

"Something's not right," I say. "I'm taking Maya up north for a week. I think we need some time apart, and you need to think about what you want."

She looks a little surprised, tilts her head to the side, and pauses for a moment. "Okay, that's fine."

I stare at her, expecting her to say more, but she doesn't. While I'm waiting I realize I have no idea what else to say either. We barely talk to each other anymore. We've forgotten how.

That evening, the sun sets in a blaze of colors, and I watch it from the front porch of our house in Healdsburg. We bought the place a few years ago, close to where we got married, thinking we'd keep it forever and retire here. The brilliant reds, yellows, and oranges of the evening sky contrast with the green trees around the property: a spectacular sight. I can't enjoy the scenery, though, as I talk on the phone. There is too much on my mind.

Maya is down for the night and I'm telling a friend about what is happening to me, to my marriage. I'm hopeful he has some advice.

"Sorry to hear this is happening, J," he says. "If you really think she's seeing someone, why don't you just track her phone?"

"Oh my god. That's brilliant. I'm going to do that now."

I hang up, run inside, and grab my laptop. I know Anne Marie's password so I log into her account, so hastily that I don't even prepare myself for what I might see. Sure enough, there on the screen is a little blue dot showing where her phone is, at a restaurant.

They are eating dinner together. A vision flashes into my head of the two of them sitting at a small table, talking, laughing, and drinking wine together. My stomach starts to twist into knots.

Obsessed, I check every few minutes until, eventually, the little blue dot moves to the highway. I watch as it makes its way into a residential neighborhood and then stops in front of a house. His house, I assume. I refresh the browser a million times over the next few hours, but the little blue dot doesn't move. At one point, I call Anne Marie, but she doesn't answer. I text her. No reply. Finally, I sit back in my chair, defeated. It is late and Maya will be up early; I have to get to bed. I tell myself that if the little blue dot hasn't moved by the morning, then I will have my answer.

I barely sleep that night; my mind races with all the possible explanations. The *what-ifs*. The *then-whats*. In the morning, a bright-eyed Maya, just over a week from her one-year birthday, wakes me. She peers over the top of her crib, bouncing and eager for me to get her out so she can start her day. I feel so grateful that she is there to take my mind off the drama that is unfolding with Anne Marie. I'm not sure how I would have put one foot in front of the other that morning if she hadn't been there, demanding that I stay present with her. I make breakfast for us and then take her for a stroller ride around the rural roads nearby. We play on the floor with blocks for a while back at the house, and then she goes down for her morning nap.

In the kitchen, I pour myself another cup of coffee and log into my computer to see where Anne Marie is. The little blue dot hasn't moved. The implications are clear. I text her: *Give me a call when you have a minute this morning.*

We don't connect until Maya's afternoon nap. When we do, my only focus is on getting her to admit what she is doing.

"Anne Marie, after all of these months of me not working, and trying to spend more time with you and Maya, something doesn't feel right," I start the call. "Now I'm home, and you aren't. You seem so distant. Is there something you aren't telling me?"

"No, J. There is nothing I'm not telling you. This has all been really confusing for me. I know you've been more present, but you can't just expect to walk back into my life and for me to drop everything and go back to how things were before. It really hurt me when you kind of disappeared. You were working all the time... and you were just...gone...for over a year!"

There is anger rising in her voice, and I'm not sure what to say. Yes, I *had* disappeared on her. It was true. And so, I realize, she must have gone looking for an emotional connection somewhere else.

"Are you sure that's all?" I ask. "I mean, if there's something going on that you want to tell me, you can. Let's be honest with each other."

As soon as I say this, I am struck by my words. I'm asking her to be honest with me, but I already know I have no intention of being honest with her about my past indiscretions. Regardless, I can't bear the thought of continuing in the state we are in. We have to break this open. We have been stagnant for far too long, and I really want us to start moving forward again, no matter what that looks like. I can handle the pain. Maybe I even deserve it. What I can't handle is this in-between state.

I can't hold back any longer. "Are you having an affair, Anne Marie?"

"What? No! I'm not having an affair." Then, in a defiant and accusatory tone, she adds: "Are you having an affair, J?"

"No. I'm not having an affair. Let's not make this about me."

"Then what makes you think I am?"

Unwilling to reveal my sources, I continue to build lies on top of lies.

"A friend of mine saw you and Bradley having dinner together last night. If there is something going on with you two, please just tell me. This whole thing is confusing for me too."

There is a long silence.

"Are you having an affair with Bradley?" I ask outright.

Again, the line is silent. I know the answer, but I need to hear her say it.

"What if I am?" she eventually asks, quietly.

And there it is. Once again Anne Marie reveals that she is the braver of the two of us.

At first, I am in shock. This just isn't something I could ever have imagined her doing.

"Wow." It is all I can muster.

She admits she is having an affair, and that it has been going on for "at least a few months." She also makes it clear that she is not ready to end that relationship. She talks about how distant we have grown, and she is apologetic that she let things get to this point. I admit that I have, indeed, been distant, but also say it will be difficult for us to try working things out if she isn't willing to end her other relationship. It is a long conversation, and it's the most honest conversation we've had in a very long time.

While I can understand why she entered into an affair, I can't accept the idea that she isn't willing to end it. And while she empathizes with my confusion, she remains firm in her resolve. I am only hearing about this now, but she has been living with this reality for a while, and she has already thought it through a hundred times.

The more she talks, the more dots my brain connects. No wonder she didn't care when I said I was quitting my job. No wonder her only question for my therapist was if the point of therapy was always to keep the couple together. She moved on a long time ago. I was her past, and he was her future. I had missed all the signs. *When was she planning to tell me?*

CHAPTER 7

"Be at least as interested in what goes on inside you as what happens outside. If you get the inside right, the outside will fall into place. Primary reality is within, secondary reality without."

—ECKHART TOLLE, *The Power of Now*

JUNE 2010

IT IS MID-MORNING, AND I'M WALKING DOWN THE TAN hall of an office building in Corte Madera, a fifteen-minute drive north of San Francisco. I'm here to meet with a "life coach," even though I have no idea what a "life coach" is.

It's been a month since Anne Marie revealed her affair. An agonizing four weeks. Once her relationship came to light, we each told our therapists, and they recommended a *third* therapist that we began seeing for joint sessions.

In one of these joint sessions, Anne Marie reveals that her relationship with Bradley started eighteen months ago, soon after we found out we were pregnant. I'm staggered when I hear that. Speechless.

An eighteen-month affair? That isn't an affair, that is a relationship! Anne Marie was having a full blown second relationship!

Somehow, I convince myself that her transgression is so much worse than all of mine *combined*. Like somewhere in the universal marriage math, a really *long* affair is worse than a bunch of one-night hookups plus a *short* affair. *I stopped cheating a year ago, and she's still doing it. My transgressions are all behind me, in my past, but hers has come to light and she refuses to end it. I'm the one who quit my job and started therapy to try to save our marriage. She let me do that and take the blame, all the while knowing she was in a new relationship and moving on, without telling me. That has to be worse than what I did, right?*

Anne Marie moves into her own apartment the next week, and starts working part-time to pay her rent. Maya moves back and forth between our places, staying with me on the days Anne Marie works.

Armed with a sense of righteous indignation, I call my family and friends to tell them what is happening.

"Oh my gosh, J," my sister says. "I'm so sorry."

I get the same sympathy from everyone else I tell, and I lap it up. Of course I never tell any of them about what *I've* done. As far as I'm concerned, that is the distant past now, and it doesn't need to be mentioned.

At a dinner one night with two friends, Mike and Julie, I share more details of the story. "So now we have a third therapist," I explain, "which seems insane. She's really nice, but we are in such a tangled mess that I have no idea how we're going to get out."

"I know this woman in Marin," Julie responds. "She's not a therapist; she's a life coach. She isn't for everyone, but she kind of specializes in helping people in times of crisis or transition. Maybe you should talk to her."

I take another bite of my pasta while I consider it. "Sure. Why not?"

And now I'm in this office building. I find the right door, open it, and enter the waiting room. It is very simple: a desk, a chair, and a small couch to sit on while I wait. I look at a painting on the wall of a beautiful landscape that has a modern edge. It evokes a sense of tranquility, and the soft sound of a water fountain adds an extra layer of serenity. The overhead fluorescent lights are off, and the only light is coming from a small lamp in the corner. Compared to the bright sun outside and the bright lights in the hallway, it seems dark in here. The woman who I scheduled with, Natalie, told me to stay in the waiting room, so I do as instructed. Normally I would check my phone for something to distract myself, but this place is peaceful, and I find myself content to stare at the painting on the wall and listen to the soothing sounds of the water.

I've been talking to my private therapist for six months, and a joint therapist with Anne Marie for a month. I have no idea how this life coach is going to help me, but at this point I'm willing to try anything. Part of me wants to try working things out with Anne Marie, but part of me thinks there is just too much damage, and we'd be better off getting divorced and starting over. Either path seems impossible, and it's starting to feel like I'm in some kind of never-ending limbo. Maybe the life coach can at least point me in a specific direction.

In the days when I have Maya, she takes my mind off things, but in the days when I'm alone I increasingly feel confused and like I'm losing hope. I've fully convinced myself by this point that Anne Marie's refusal to end her affair is much worse than anything I've done. My cheating is in the past. Our marriage is at risk of dissolving *now*, so it is her fault. It is all her fault.

The door at the other side of the room bursts open and a woman emerges. "Oh hi! You must be Jason."

"Yes, hi." I am awkward, very unsure of myself.

"I'm Melissa." She extends her hand. She is bright and animated, and behind her a beam of sunlight streams out of her office into the quiet waiting room. "C'mon in." She gestures to me to come into the room. I follow her direction, and she closes the door behind us. From that moment forward, my life will never be the same.

* * *

ONCE INSIDE HER OFFICE, I see the source of the morning sunshine through a large east-facing window. The aesthetic is consistent in here: modern and straightforward, but very comfortable and serene.

"You get the comfy one." She points to a couch with pillows in shades of greens and purples, which match the painting of another landscape on the wall, by an artist I later learn is Astrid Preston.

As I sit and try to get comfortable, I start to get nervous. Scanning the room, I realize there are no college degrees hanging on the walls. Apparently, credentials are important to me, something I hadn't discovered until this moment. *I wonder where this woman went to school?*

"So," she interrupts my thoughts as she sits in her chair across from me, "tell me what's happening." She grabs a notebook and pen off the carpeted floor as I begin my well-rehearsed story.

"Well, about six months ago, I realized my marriage was failing so I quit my job to stay home and try to repair my relationship with my wife."

Translation: *I saw things were going south so I quit my job to try to fix it. Aren't I such a good guy?*

"But things didn't get better," I continue. "Actually, they got worse."

"I see." She scribbles some notes.

"Then about a six weeks ago, I found out my wife, Anne Marie, was having an affair. And when I confronted her about it, she said she wasn't ready to end that relationship. So, she moved out a few weeks ago. We've been seeing therapists—three actually: a private one for each of us and another woman we have joint sessions with, and that seems to be helping, but I'm really not sure where all of this is going."

Translation: *And wouldn't you know, my wife was having an affair, and she doesn't want to end it?! And I'm going to therapists so I'm trying to hold our marriage together. See? I'm a good guy.*

"Mmm hmm." She scribbles more.

"So...that's it, I guess?"

Translation: *Um, this is the part where you're supposed to feel sorry for me. Are you feeling sorry for me? Because I can't tell. If you are, please amp it up.*

Melissa's pen wobbles back and forth over her notepad. I sit in a mildly awkward silence. Everyone else I told that story to said some version of, "Oh you poor thing!" Maybe she's still digesting it.

Eventually, she looks up at me. "Okay, so I'm not sure how much Julie told you about what I do, but I'm not a therapist. I'm a coach. The goal of this"—she points to herself, then me—"is not to sit and talk to you every week for the rest of your life. I want to help you get well and then after you get well, we will end our coaching sessions and you will move on. Does that make sense?"

"Sure. Yes."

Translation: *Maybe she'll feel sorry for me after I tell her how hard I was working to support our family. I should get to that part soon.*

"Also," she continues, "I didn't go to any fancy schools, and you can't find any information about me on the internet. My schedule is packed, I have a line of people waiting to get in, and I don't need to promote myself publicly."

Totally true, I thought. I had tried to research her before my appointment and couldn't find anything about her online, which struck me as odd.

"That's fine," I say.

"We meet once a week for an hour, and I will give you assignments to do on your own between sessions. I ask people to commit to at least ten sessions so I know they will take it seriously and we can build some momentum. Does all of that sound good?"

"Yes, that all makes sense." She is much more energetic than any therapist I have talked to. There is a plan and a process. She has a spark in her, and she has my attention.

"Okay, let's get started." She puts down her notebook and pen and looks straight at me. I struggle to maintain the eye contact. "So, your energy right now feels like a victim."

She pauses, presumably to read my reaction to what she's said.

"Okay," I drawl out.

Translation: *Yes! Bingo! I am a victim! You are good, lady.*

"The first thing I want to tell you, Jason, is that you are not a victim. Somehow, you have created this situation for yourself. I'm going to help you figure out why."

I blink at her. *I'm not a victim? Uh, yes, I am! My wife has been having an affair for a year and a half, refuses to end it, and it is driving our marriage apart. If you look up the word "victim" in the dictionary, that is the definition, and there is a picture of me.*

"Have you been feeling like a victim?" she asks.

"Yes, yes I have." I sit up a little straighter. Now I'm on firmer footing.

"Tell me how."

"Well, I don't think it's my fault that Anne Marie has been having an affair for so long. It was her choice to do that. And it isn't my fault that she refuses to end her relationship with this guy. She's the one making those decisions. So yeah, I do feel like a victim."

"Have you talked to anyone about what's happening?"

"Yes, I've talked to my parents about it, and my close friends."

"What do they think about it?"

"Well, they're all really surprised. Aside from a few typical break-ups in college, Anne Marie and I have been together for almost fifteen years, so my family and friends all know her well, and they are surprised that she would do something like this. It's so unlike her."

"Do they feel bad for you?"

"Of course they do. They've been very supportive of me since all of this happened."

"Tell me a little bit about your parents." She picks up her pen and notebook again.

I proceed to tell her about my mom and dad, their divorce when I was young, being raised by my mother and stepfather.

"Where did you grow up?" she asks.

"In the suburbs of New Jersey."

"Do you have siblings?"

"Yes, one sister, five years older than me."

More questions come at me, rapid fire.

"What do you do for work?"

"How did you and Anne Marie meet?"

"Where did she grow up?"

"What is her family like?"

There are several more. We are not making eye contact; she is looking at her notebook and scribbling the whole time. She reminds me of a computer, gathering raw data. Finally, she puts down her pen and notebook and looks at me again. Again, I fight hard not to break the eye contact.

"I know what's happening here," she says. "I coach relationships and affairs all day long, so I know where to take you. Ready?"

I don't think I am. She hasn't felt sorry for me yet, so I'm a little disoriented. *Usually people feel sorry for me by now. What the fuck, lady?* But her confidence is like a freight train, pushing us forward. I can tell that we're building momentum and that there isn't much I can do to stop it. I swallow hard. "Yes, I'm ready." For some reason, I trust her.

She explains how important it is for me to take responsibility for everything that happens in my life. "You didn't make the decision for Anne Marie to have an affair," she says at one point, "but you created the conditions in your life where that could happen to you."

Her words pierce right through me. It's as if she knows I had been cheating on Anne Marie. *How does she know that? I have to get back on script.*

"I was working hard to support our family," I say, righteousness in my voice. "I had a lot of responsibility, and I had to work long hours to get my job done."

"Did Anne Marie force you to work those long hours?"

"No, I guess she didn't. But I was doing that for us, for our family."

Translation: *You've got this all wrong. I'm the good guy here!*

"Well, that's just another way of saying that it wasn't your choice. Was that all really just for your family? Could some of it have been for you?"

Okay, now you're stepping over the line. Nobody challenges my work ethic.

Our sparring escalates and continues for the rest of the hour. At first, I remain resistant to—no, incensed by—her suggestion that I am somehow responsible for what happened between Anne Marie and me. But she stands firm, and her reasoning is impenetrable. Every statement she makes is like a razor that cuts through all of my bullshit. I have never experienced anything like it. I'm not used to being in a conversation where I can't control the narrative. As she continues to obliterate my typical defenses, I gradually realize the foundation underneath my arguments is filled with cracks. It has no integrity.

She wears me down. If I was unnerved at the start, at the end I am downright wobbly. But then, something inside me cracks open a little. A tiny, tiny sliver of humility sneaks out, and I admit, "I guess maybe I did have something to do with Anne Marie's affair."

Once she sees me taking even the tiniest amount of responsibility for what happened, she is quick to point out the benefits of doing so.

"If you take responsibility for everything that happens in your life, you'll realize you also have the ability to decide what you do next."

And with that simple statement she gives me something I hadn't had in many months: hope. She helps me see that for the last six months I'd been waiting for Anne Marie to decide what happens with our relationship. I now realize I don't have to sit and wait, like a victim. I can have a voice here too. Suddenly, I am empowered.

During the discussion she also makes educated guesses about my relationship with Anne Marie, and the relationships that we each have with our respective parents. I am amazed at how accurate she is. She has only just met me and hasn't even met Anne Marie, much less either of our parents. Yet when she guesses things they might say, or ways they might act, she is exactly on the mark. I am transfixed.

We end with a brief discussion of how important it is for me to be completely open and honest if I'm going to get the most out of my work with her.

"The truth speeds everything up," she says. "Don't be afraid of the truth." She then gives me an assignment. "Think about all of your secrets and write them down so we can start talking about them next week."

Oh shit. How does she know I have secrets?

Before I have time to worry about that, our session time ends. We stand, and she says, "I'm going to introduce a lot of new concepts to you, and you may feel differently about certain things in a few months than you do today. Can you agree that you won't make any major decisions for at least two to three months?"

"Major decisions about Anne Marie?

"About anything."

It feels like an odd request, but so far I trust her, so I agree.

I depart her office and walk down the hall toward the elevator, feeling different, energized. On the way in, I was sulking and confused. Now I'm excited and hopeful. In fact, I feel so hopeful that I call Anne Marie when I get in my car, to tell her about my session with Melissa.

"Hello," she answers.

"Hi."

There is a slightly awkward silence. We aren't talking often, mostly just in our joint therapy sessions or to coordinate Maya's schedule. I'm only guessing our lines of communication are open enough for this.

"Hey, I'm sorry to disturb you, but I just got out of my session with that life coach Julie introduced me to, and there are some things I wanted to share with you."

"Oh, sure." Her voice doesn't sound like she's just being polite. "Like what?"

I tell her what Melissa said about our relationship. What she guessed about my parents. What she guessed about Anne Marie and her own parents. "She also helped me see that I need to take some responsibility for what has happened between us, and I'm going to work on that."

"Wow," she says. "You got all of that out of one session? Maybe I should talk to this woman too."

CHAPTER 8

"One does not accumulate but eliminate.
It is not daily increase but daily decrease.
The height of cultivation always runs to simplicity."

—BRUCE LEE

JUNE 2011

IT IS EARLY ON A FOGGY SAN FRANCISCO SATURDAY morning. I sit on a bench near Chrissy Field, watching the cargo ships roll in and out of the bay and listening to the fog horns on the bridge. I come here for walks or runs a few times a week now, and it is a good place to gather myself.

The last year has been a roller-coaster. After Anne Marie started talking to Melissa, we both stopped seeing our therapists, and now we both talk to Melissa every week. It is unusual for someone in Melissa's position to work with both sides of a couple in distress, but something about her approach works for us. Early on, she made it clear that she would never pick sides. "I don't care if you guys get divorced or stay together," she told us. "My job is to help you both be healthy, whole individuals. Once you get well, it won't matter if you stay together or divorce; it will be beautiful either way."

The work with her is brutal, like a hard workout at the gym. You know you'll feel good when it's over, but it's painful to get through. She has a series of verbal "tools" that seem to bore deep into my subconscious and touch parts of me that have been hidden for decades. I often leave sessions feeling so braindead I can barely speak for a few hours. In one particularly memorable session a few months after we started, I find myself sobbing uncontrollably after I touch the hurt I felt as a boy when my parents divorced and my dad moved halfway across the country.

As a father potentially headed for divorce myself, I would never dream of leaving Maya. "My dad left me," I cry. "How could he have left me?" When it surfaced, I didn't even know those feelings were buried inside me. I had been carrying that hurt around for thirty years. Thirty! *What else is buried in there?*

Week after week, month after month, Melissa challenges me to dig deeper, and I keep going back for more. In addition to our sessions, she has a huge arsenal of material, and she seems to know exactly what to prescribe at exactly the right moment. I read every book she tells me to. I listen to every guided meditation. I don't understand what the work is doing to me, but gradually I feel different. I feel more solid. More honest. I'm still having trouble being alone, however, and contrary to her advice, I go through two dating relationships, each lasting a few months. But I'm honest with Anne Marie about them while they are happening, which feels like an improvement.

Occasionally Anne Marie and I have joint sessions together, and those are the most interesting. At times it is a dialogue between all of us; at other times Melissa focuses on helping one of us through a difficult issue while the other just sits in silence and watches the processing. Anne Marie and I are raw and more vulnerable in these sessions than we've ever been, with anyone, in our lives. There are a lot of tears from both of us.

Anne Marie is still in her relationship with Bradley, but I'm more at peace with that now. We've had alternating periods of closeness and distance over the last year. When we are most distant, it is Maya who continually brings us back together. We have to share time with her, and we have to coordinate schedules. To this day I remain convinced that if Maya had not been there fighting for us to stay together, we would have drifted apart. Drifting apart would have been easier than doing the work we each had to do on ourselves, and a big part of what motivated each of us to do our hard work was a desire to be the best parents for Maya that we could be.

Working with the same coach gives us a common vocabulary, and sometimes after one of us drops Maya off, we have long conversations on the couch and share what we are learning in our work. In her private sessions with Melissa, Anne Marie is experiencing similar breakthroughs as I am. We start connecting dots around where things went wrong in our relationship. In those moments it feels like we are back in college together, talking and listening, getting to know each other. We become friends again; we go on a few ski trips together and spend a day sailing in the bay. It is all platonic. Maybe this is our fate. We will always be connected by Maya and by the past we share together, but maybe our future is as friends and co-parents. It is different than what we expected, but that doesn't mean it's bad.

My relationship with Anne Marie isn't the only thing that takes me back to my youth. Since we began sharing Maya after Anne Marie moved out, I've taken advantage of the times when I'm not on dad duty to do things with friends. I go mountain biking and surfing with Pete. Once a week I get up early and do a long trail run with Todd. A few times a month I meet Matt for nine holes of golf, and one weekend we drive up to Sacramento for a rock concert. I start to feel like I did in my last year of high school and first years of college. That was an amazing time in my life. I was on the straight and narrow after my drug bust, I had a great group of friends and was madly in love with Anne Marie, and I was working hard at my grades. I was building a new future for myself, and it feels like that is happening again. I am hopeful. I feel fresher somehow. I'm more optimistic that everything is going to turn out all right for me.

That guy who I was back then, he was a good guy. I haven't liked myself in a long time, but when I remember the guy I was in those years, I like him. I miss him. I want to get back in touch with him. I had taken a detour from the path he was on, but maybe I could go back to where the paths had diverged and start over in a new direction this time.

In addition to encouraging me to stay single (so I could focus on working on myself), Melissa also encourages me to simplify my life in other ways. "You've been efforting your way through life, Jason," she tells me. "I promise there is a way to create just as much abundance for yourself with much less effort."

I have no idea what she is talking about, and frankly, I'm a little offended. Challenging my work ethic is like challenging me at the core. "I've gotten where I am because of how hard I've worked. I can't just sit on the couch all day and meditate. Monks don't have mortgages."

She laughs. "Trust me on this one, Jason."

With every passing month, I do trust her more, so I'm willing to give it a try. I start simplifying my life. With her help, I identify things and relationships in my life that I don't want anymore, and I let go of, or "subtract" them. I learn that we all do a great job of gathering and collecting. We collect things, projects, responsibilities, and relationships, but we don't do a good job of subtracting those things once they aren't serving us anymore. I start giving away things and clothes I don't use or wear. I stop watching television completely. I unsubscribe from email mailing lists. I say *No* to most invitations. I finish projects that I'm working on, but I'm more selective about what new projects I start. Slowly, gradually, more space opens up in my life. And more time. Like time to sit on this bench and watch the bay for a while. I never used to sit still for something like this. I was always rushing around, so proud of how busy I was. Being busy was one of the ways I showed the world how successful I was. It was a badge of honor. But I'm learning that busy was just a way to keep running. To never have to be present with anyone. To never have to just be, alone, with myself. To not have to feel anything.

* * *

ABOUT SIX MONTHS AGO, WHEN Anne Marie and I were at a particular low point and I was convinced we were heading for divorce, I got a job to give me something to focus on besides my marriage. I had also burned through a lot of savings by that point, which eventually had to stop. *Subtraction* becomes my new personal mantra at work. I focus only on the essential things I need to do, and surprisingly, I am much more productive with much less effort. I even help my direct reports do the same thing in their own work, and they thrive. Melissa is right. There is a way to create more with less effort. It's a new way of working, of living for me. More importantly, going back into a work environment, surrounded by new people, helps me see just how much I have changed in the year since I left Palantir. The way I interact with people and approach my work is completely different. I am different.

I can change. There is hope for me.

A few weeks later, Anne Marie tells me in a phone call that she is ending her relationship with Bradley.

"But I'm not ready to be together with you again, J," she adds. "I'm learning that I need some time alone, to get to know myself and what I want."

"I understand." I do. We are going through very similar processes. As difficult as it is for me, I have to stay patient.

Months tick by, and Melissa continues taking a wrecking ball to my life. "Your foundation isn't solid, Jason," she tells me one day. "We have to tear down everything you built on top of it, excavate the foundation, and then pour a new one. Then you can start building again, with integrity."

I still haven't told her about porn or my cheating in the past, yet she talks to me about integrity all the time. It's like she knows there are things I'm not telling her. But I have so much work to do, it doesn't matter. She has plenty of material to work with.

As I continue to change, I realize I don't like my job anymore, and so that fall, about a year after I'd started, I leave. Melissa encourages me to take time off before I jump into a new job.

"A job is like a relationship. If you get right back into another job before you take time to grow, it's going to be the same cycle over and over again."

I have learned so much from her by now that again, I trust her. I decide I want to take time off to continue working on myself before I look for another job. Even better, I'm going to get away to the mountains somewhere. Soul searching in the mountains sounds cliché, but it also sounds appealing. Plus, I'll be able to ski, an activity I've enjoyed since my late teen years. It feels like the perfect way to keep getting to know that guy I was back then; the guy I still very much want to reconnect with.

I bring the idea up with Anne Marie on the phone.

"I think I want to go live in a ski town for the winter, before I get another job," I start. "But I'm not sure what to do about Maya. It will probably be for three months. Do I take her with me? Do we trade off monthly, or every few weeks?"

We discuss it for a while and then Anne Marie asks, "What if I just come with you?" There is a long moment of silence on the phone. Once again, Maya has pulled us closer together.

I hadn't even considered this option. Anne Marie ended her relationship with Bradley many months ago, but she has been clear that she is not ready to get back together with me. Could that be changing?

"Sure!" I'm unable to contain my excitement. "That would be great!"

We spend the next few months in a whirlwind of activity: picking a town to move to, finding a place to live, and moving Anne Marie out of her apartment. After a year and a half of therapy, coaching, and soul searching, we are a team again. Similar to our years just after graduating college, we don't know exactly where our relationship is going; we just know that we are best friends, heading out for another adventure together. Anne Marie summarizes her feelings in an email to me on the day she gives her landlord her move-out notice:

The deed is done. Alrighty Portnoy...I'm having a hard time breathing but I have faith that everything is going to work out just fine. :-)

A month later, in early January, we load Maya and our gear into our cars and point them both east on Highway 80 for the long drive to Park City, Utah. It is a crisp but beautiful sunny day. Anne Marie has Maya in her car just ahead of me on the highway, and I watch them snaking through the Sierra Nevada mountains near Lake Tahoe. As we exit California, the wide expanse of the Nevada desert opens up before us. I see a completely new landscape. A new future. *I'm getting a second chance. This is my opportunity to start fresh, and I'm not going to screw this up.*

But as I had learned as an exchange student in college, changing locations doesn't change a person. And eventually I would learn that you can only start fresh after you've brought complete closure to your past. I had done a lot of work in therapy and coaching, and I legitimately had changed quite a bit. But I still hadn't shared any details about my pornography habit or my past philandering with anyone. My lack of honesty with Melissa meant there was a limit to how deep I could go in my work with her, and that meant there was a limit to how much I could really grow.

Anne Marie, on the other hand, had been an open book—completely honest about her affair. She was really doing deep work on herself, and growing and changing a lot as a result. Her willingness to join me on this latest adventure was her way of telling me that she trusts me. But have I really changed enough to deserve that trust?

CHAPTER 9

"...but beneath the surface is a little child who feels empty and needy, a child whose needs are insatiable because he has a child's needs in an adult body. This insatiable child is the core of all compulsive/addictive behavior."

—JOHN BRADSHAW, *Healing the Shame that Binds You*

JULY 2013

I STAND IN AN OPEN FIELD, ADMIRING THE MOUNTAIN scenery in the distance. The cloudless sky is deep blue, and the contrast with the green trees and the yellow field grasses paints a beautiful picture right in front of me. The Utah sun is warm on my skin, and I close my eyes and take a deep inhale to try to breathe this moment in. I am warm. This feels like home.

My moment is interrupted by the sound of an engine starting. I open my eyes and see the excavator slowly coming to life. Today it will start digging a big hole in the ground. A foundation for a new home that Anne Marie and I are building.

In the last eighteen months, Park City has been everything our family needed it to be. When we arrived, we didn't know anyone, and our family spent the winter months sequestered in a little condo, playing in the heavy blanket of Utah snow, or giggling over cups of hot cocoa. We were together. We were healing. Anne Marie and I were getting closer again. One night in the first spring, after Maya was in bed, we found ourselves on the couch in a deep conversation.

"Do you think we can go back to the way things were before?" Anne Marie asked.

I consider the question before answering. "No. I don't." I paused again, struggling to put my feelings into words. "We are different people now. And maybe that's a good thing. The way things were before wasn't actually that good. It may have seemed good on the outside, but it wasn't good on the inside." I shifted in my seat to look more directly at her. "We can't go back to who we were then. We have to go forward as the people we are today. It will be different, but I think it will be even better than it was before."

I was so hopeful. So confident. And part of it was true. After what we'd gone through and what we'd learned in our coaching work, we really *were* new people. We were no longer the starry-eyed kids we had been ten years earlier when we got married. We were different now. We'd been through the marital equivalent of a war (or natural disaster?). We had wounds and we had scars, but we had survived, and we knew more.

Shortly after that conversation on the couch, Anne Marie and I decided to stay in Park City permanently. She felt it would be a great environment for raising Maya. I liked the lower income taxes and cost of living. In hindsight, it was neither of those things, and nothing we could have identified consciously. The reasons we were drawn to stay had everything to do with how we felt deep inside. Here, we weren't haunted by our pasts. Here we had space to become new people. Here we had a place to start over.

Maya started school and we signed her up for dance lessons at a local studio. In the fall of that year Anne Marie started her own business making organic, cold-pressed juices. A few months later, I started my own business, a venture capital fund. By the end of the year, we were drawing up plans for a new home and thinking about when we might like to welcome a new baby into our family.

A new place. New jobs. A new home. A new family. It was a new beginning. Only it wasn't.

* * *

I HAVE BEEN ON GOOD behavior for a long time, but my porn habit is still there, simmering just below the surface. In truth, at that time of my life, I still didn't consider it a problem. I had reevaluated the areas of my life that seemed to blind me in the past, but most of that revolved around my relationship to my work and the importance of making money. To me, porn remained just something that all guys did. So what's the problem?

The problem is, I *still* don't understand that porn is a drug for me. Actually, it is more than just a drug, it is a *gateway drug*. Porn is a portal into a dark world. A world of lies. A world of guilt. A world of shame. By continuing to look at porn, even only occasionally, I am continuing to dance with the dark. And gradually, the dark starts to pull me back in.

Any entrepreneur knows that starting a new business is hard work, and our two businesses are no exception. Anne Marie is in bed early every night so she can wake up before dawn to make juices. To get my fund off the ground, I am up late working on my laptop and traveling back to San Francisco frequently for meetings. Once again, we are ships passing in the night. Most nights I quietly climb into bed while she is already asleep, and then she quietly departs around five in the morning while I am still snoozing. Working late on my laptop. Frequent business trips. Past behaviors coupled with new opportunities, and old habits came back to life.

* * *

THE FIRST TIME I SEE an advertisement for Ashley Madison on a porn site I am struck by the brutality of their slogan: *Life is short. Have an affair.* There it is. Out in the open. Not just out in the open, they are *encouraging* me to have an affair. As I click through the pages my jaw drops. Forget the old days of Craigslist, or even escorts. Here are hundreds, no *thousands*, of young women with profiles advertising their willingness to have affairs with married men. After a few more clicks around the web I learn there are other sites like it, and one called "SeekingArrangement" resonates most with me.

At the time, SeekingArrangement is an online "dating" website that helps attractive young women or men ("sugar babies") find wealthy, older men and women ("sugar daddies" and "sugar mammas") who want to financially support them in exchange for their...availability. There is no ambiguity on the website. Sugar baby listings, complete with pictures, body size stats, and life desires, are very clear about the financial *assistance* they require and the frequency of their *availability*. Sugar daddy profiles are similarly clear about how much money they are willing to spend and what kind of availability they expect in return. The site fuels a classic fantasy power dynamic, where men can feel like they are "taking care" of a woman, and it draws me in.

While I am a diligent student with Melissa, Anne Marie is the star pupil in our class. I still keep secrets; she does not. All of her *stuff* is out in the open and fodder for her to work on. She is busily excavating her cracked foundation and pouring a new one. Starting her business is the external manifestation of the progress she is making in her internal work. She is building a new edifice on top of her new, sturdier, platform. As she does, it becomes clearer that she really doesn't need me. If I harbor any masculine stereotypes in my head about being the man of the house, or taking care of her and Maya in some way, she systematically smashes those notions, one at a time. This is not something we talk about; it just happens quietly under the surface.

As she builds her business, her confidence grows, and any dependencies she may have had on me start to wither. She doesn't need my advice for how to talk to the lawyers or accountants anymore. She doesn't need my help making a spreadsheet to figure something out. Really, she would be just fine without me. She is becoming the "whole and healthy person" that Melissa said was her goal for us three years ago. But I'm not becoming "whole and healthy."

My foundation still has cracks and holes that need to be filled. I need to feel needed. I need to feel wanted. I need attention. Here are thousands of young women advertising their willingness to give me what I need. *Yes, SeekingArrangement, I am seeking something. I am seeking attention.*

Even though these needs are out of sight of my conscious mind, I still have plenty of old justifications and entitlements close enough to the surface, and they all come flooding back. *I'm a successful man. I need sex and I deserve it. This is just what men do.* And as odd as it may sound, the sheer scale of the websites—millions of users!—somehow gives me the feeling that what I am doing is, well, normal.

Within weeks I have set up a profile and I'm interviewing young women in Salt Lake City or, for my business trips, in San Francisco. Out of concern for my safety, I always insist that we meet at a coffee shop or bar first. Some of the interviews never go beyond that first meeting, but many end in motel rooms. Or in their apartments. Or in my car, parked in a dark corner of a parking garage. One girl from SeekingArrangement turns out to be a Stanford student and shows up to meet me in San Francisco in a brand new Audi her father just bought her. We talk for an hour and then I send her home. She is too young. Another young woman and I get close to the "relationship" model that SeekingArrangement is peddling. She is an artist in her late-twenties, and we meet several times over the course of six months, me flying her to various cities to meet me while I'm on business trips.

The excitement of the chase and the rush of the act fuel my ego, and for brief moments, in the midst of the action, I feel wanted. But afterward, when my ego is numb from its drugs, the deeper part of myself always feels more hollow and lonelier than before. Alone. Empty. Guilty. Ashamed. I don't have the awareness to understand what is happening to me, but with every encounter I am destroying a small part of myself. I am making the cracks in my foundation bigger and bigger, which only drives me deeper into the behavior that is destroying me. It is a vicious cycle, but I am so deep in it, I can't see it.

As time passes, while Anne Marie continues to stand more on her own two feet, my needs become insatiable. Eventually, the women from SeekingArrangement just aren't enough. I start going to massage parlors on a regular basis. I meet a woman in the hallway of my hotel one night during a business trip to Chicago. She is also married, yet somehow we wind up in her bed the next day. One night, in San Francisco, I go to a strip club and invite a dancer to hang out after her shift ends. She calls me at two in the morning and we arrange to meet. I never talk to her again after that night.

In a very risky move, I hit on Maya's babysitter, who, thankfully, has the good sense to reject my proposal. The dialogue in my head after the conversation—*That was* really *stupid! What are you thinking?!*—doesn't go far enough for me to realize that I'm *not* thinking. I am being driven by deep parts of myself I can't see. Low level animal desires. I am a predator now. Once again, I'm out of control.

And then, just like in high school, I finally cry out for help loud enough to be heard.

* * *

ALMOST A YEAR AFTER BREAKING ground on our home, on a sunny spring day in May 2014, I find myself walking down a side street in the Mission District of San Francisco. I'm on the phone talking to Ed, the CEO of one of our fund's early-stage portfolio companies. We used to talk every week, but for the last five to six weeks our calls kept getting canceled because he's been so busy. A lot can happen in an early-stage company in that timeframe, so I am eager to catch up with him.

He tells me about the latest product features they are releasing, and I'm excited about all the progress they've made. But then there is an awkward pause, and the energy of the conversation shifts.

"So, listen, this is pretty awkward for me," he starts, "but did you hang out with Leslie back in January?"

I stop and stare at the sidewalk. Leslie is an employee at Ed's company. *So this is why he's been cancelling our calls.*

"Yeah." I clear my throat. "Yeah, I did."

"Yeah." He's quiet for a few seconds. "She's pretty upset about it."

My heart skips a beat and I get tunnel vision. Then I can't hear anything. A gaggle of school kids rush past me on the sidewalk, but my brain barely registers the commotion. *I'm fucked.*

Another long pause. "I'm really sorry, Ed. It was really stupid of me."

"Yeah." I can tell he's trying to pick his words carefully.

"How did it come up?" Then, before he can answer, "*When* did it come up?"

"She brought it up about a month ago. Said the whole thing made her feel really uncomfortable. We took it seriously, and we've talked about it internally and gotten advice from lawyers. I'll be honest with you, it's not a great situation, and I've been avoiding our calls because I wasn't sure what to do. I've never had to deal with anything like this before."

I'm still motionless on the sidewalk. I can't move, though my heart is racing now. Ed is a young CEO, busting his ass every day to try to build a company, take care of his employees, and generate a great outcome for their investors. Leslie is a bright young woman with an entire career and life ahead of her. They've all been hurt now because of something stupid I did. Something so irresponsible. I was supposed to be a grown up in the relationship, the more experienced venture capitalist, helping them build their company. Instead, I had been immature and created a giant distraction for all of them. I was nauseous. In a quiet voice, all I could say was, "I'm really sorry, Ed."

"Yeah, I know you are."

I flash back to the morning after the incident. I had awakened suddenly with a jolt. It was still dark outside my window, but I had sobered up enough for panic to set in immediately. *What the fuck was I doing?! How stupid can I be?! I was alone in the apartment of a young woman who works at a portfolio company, trying to convince her to have sex with me. I can't believe I did that! I have to do damage control. I have to talk to her. Oh my god, what have I done?*

I come back to reality on the sidewalk. "I talked to her on the phone the morning after," I explain. "I thought we were just two people who'd had too much to drink and gotten into an awkward situation. I had no idea it affected her so much. Do you think I should call her to apologize? Or write a letter or something?"

"No, no." His response was quick. "I don't think you should contact her. Actually, our lawyers feel like the fact that you never tried contacting her since then is probably a good thing."

"Oh, okay. What happens next?"

Ed sighs. "Honestly, I'm not sure. I think we need to have more conversations internally. I don't know what direction she wants to go with all of this. Let's just stay in touch."

As we hang up I can see the headline on some Silicon Valley news website: *Venture Capitalist hits on portfolio company employee.*

What am I doing? My business partner and I are planning trips to New York City in a few months to raise money for our second fund. If this comes out publicly it would be the end of our firm. The end of my career as a VC. And what about Anne Marie? After everything we've been through, how could I be capable of this?

If Anne Marie and I learned anything from our separation, it is that we need to be more honest with each other. I am on board with that in concept, but my *honesty* is still very selective. We actually *are* more honest with each other about things that we are thinking and feeling, but I have never come clean about my pornography or cheating. I still keep those secrets locked away in a separate, parallel life.

Because there is a risk this could come out publicly, I think it would be best if Anne Marie hears it from me. Not strong enough to remain standing while I speak to her, I find a stone wall to sit on under a tree and I dial her number.

"Good morning!" she answers, bright and full of energy. "How's your day going?"

"It's been interesting already."

"Oh. What's up?"

"Well, I did something I shouldn't have."

Her voice changes, the lightness diminished. "Like what?"

I tell her a condensed version of the story.

"I went to an event at one of our portfolio companies when I was here a few months ago. Afterward one of the employees invited me back to her apartment, and I went. I was drunk and I don't remember the details, but I know nothing sexual happened. Anyway, she is upset about it and talked to the CEO about it, and it's not really a great situation."

She takes a long time to respond.

"Wow, J."

"Yeah. I'm really sorry." I hold my head with my hand. It feels heavier and heavier with each second.

"Is that it?" she asks.

"Yes, that's the whole story."

"Has anything like this happened before?"

"No. This is the first time anything like this has happened. And I never talked to her again after that night. I feel so stupid. I'm really sorry, Anne Marie. I don't know what will happen and I wanted to be sure you heard about it from me."

"Okay." She is quiet. Processing.

She sighs, then says, "I guess we'll talk more about this when you get home."

"Yes, absolutely." I'm somewhat relieved. "I'd like to get Melissa's advice too. I have my weekly call with her in half an hour. Can I conference you in?"

"Sure."

I spend the next thirty minutes walking around the residential side streets of the Mission District thinking about what is happening. *This is bad. This is really bad. Fuck, fuck, fuck.* I can't really think much else. Everything feels so uncertain and nothing else matters in that moment.

At the appointed time, I sit on a set of shaded steps on a quiet street and dial Melissa to start our call. When she answers I tell her there is a topic I'd like to cover, and I'd like Anne Marie to join our call. Anne Marie and I have joint calls all the time, so it's not an odd request. She agrees and I conference Anne Marie in.

"Okay," I begin, then I stop to sigh. I tell Melissa the same story I told Anne Marie, complete with the same opening line, "I did something I shouldn't have..."

Eerily, she asks the same exact questions that Anne Marie asked, in the same exact order.

"Is that it?"

"Yes, that's it."

"Has anything like this happened before?"

"No, never," again I lie.

"Well, get ready. This is about to get interesting."

Her advice is that I should be honest with everyone about what happened and accept the consequences. This will be the best way to move through the experience with the least amount of pain and embarrassment for myself, Anne Marie, Leslie, and the company.

"We're going to talk about why you've created this for yourself and what you will learn from it, but right now I'm more concerned about Anne Marie," she says.

I'm not expecting her to say that, but as soon as she does it makes complete sense.

"Anne Marie?" Melissa asks. Anne Marie has been silent for the entire call so far.

"Yes," she answers.

"Are you okay if I use the rest of this hour to coach you?"

"Sure."

"Good. Jason, I will try to call you after my coaching sessions today." I know her well by now, and what's she's really saying is, "You need to sit in this for a while and take responsibility for your actions. Nobody is going to rescue you."

We end the call, and I sit on the steps for a few more minutes, my mind too blank to do anything else. Slowly, I get up and make my way to the office where I was originally heading, but when I arrive I'm so distracted I don't even want to make eye contact with anyone. I go straight to a conference room and close the door. I just need to sit in a quiet space for a minute.

Over the next few weeks, in follow up conversations with Ed, I apologize and say I will cooperate fully with any investigation or resolution that is necessary. I also explain the situation to Paul, my business partner, so that he is prepared in case it becomes a larger story.

Anne Marie and I have a lot of conversations about it when I return from San Francisco. She is very hurt. I assure her it was the first time anything like this happened and promise nothing like it will happen again. Eventually, she seems to settle into an uneasy acceptance of the situation and gradually it fades. Maybe she believes me. Or maybe she doesn't believe me, but she doesn't want to know the truth because it would be too painful. I can't be sure; I am just relieved that she drops it.

Melissa, on the other hand, does not let it go so easily.

PART 3

THIS IS REALLY ME

CHAPTER 10

"We are in love with the present man, and all the things that constitute him, and we are not prepared to slay him that the other may be born."

—DR. EMMET FOX, *The Lost Booklets of Emmet Fox*

MAY 2014

I'M ON THE PHONE IN A SESSION WITH MELISSA, AND once again she shines a spotlight into my subconscious. She knows there are parts of me I keep walled off. I know she can tell because she increasingly asks me questions I can't answer honestly, and when she does, I just get quiet.

At one point when I pause, she jumps in. "What are you thinking, Jason? Right now?" she asks, urgency in her voice.

I'm thinking about one of my lies, so I say, "Nothing. My mind is blank."

She knows it's a lie, and I know she knows. Fortunately, she keeps working with what I make available. Perhaps she knows that, eventually, the walls will come down if she just keeps shining the light.

For several weeks after the incident, she repeatedly asks if that was *really* the only time something like this has happened. She's coached marital infidelity a million times, she tells me, and she knows where there is smoke, there is probably fire.

I'm not sure if it is her persistence or the fact that the situation really *had* scared the shit out of me, but something inside me starts to shift. In the past my behavior risked damaging my relationship with Anne Marie. Now I've added professional damage to the equation, too. More importantly, I've created traumatic experiences in the lives of innocent young women. Hooking up with women advertising on websites was one thing, but the babysitter? Or the portfolio company employee? I am an older, married man. By propositioning them, I am sending them a message that supports the societal stereotypes I, myself, have fallen victim to: Men are not to be trusted. Men are predators and only after one thing. Men are weak. Or worse, I am implying that their only worth is their sexuality. How was this affecting them? And how will it influence their own relationships in the future? I don't know exactly how, but I know it isn't good.

Although I am still very asleep, the incident wakes me up just enough to see more clearly that I am moving in the wrong direction again. My behavior scares me, and I'm now hurting innocent people. I need to address this before it goes any further.

So finally, after Melissa asks yet again one day, a tiny crack forms in one of my walls.

"Yes, that's the only time I've done that, but...there is something else that's been on my mind," I start.

"Great," Melissa says. "I'm all ears."

"Man, I'm not sure how to say this. It's so embarrassing."

"Really, Jason? Embarrassing? I've coached everything. Nothing you say is going to surprise me."

"Okay. Okay." I try to hold it back, but I can't. It has to come out. "I can't stop looking at porn." The words come in a rush and deflate me.

"What? Porn?" She laughs, clearly surprised. "Did you say *porn*?" Her emphasis on the word makes me cringe.

Cringe because, in all these years, aside from the one time I brought it up with Anne Marie, I have never talked openly about this with anyone. Cringe because, somewhere inside, I know that this will mark the beginning of a big change in my life, and I'm afraid of that uncertain future.

"Yes, porn. This is so embarrassing to say, but I can't stop looking at porn!" I exclaim, almost excitedly. Actually, I *am* excited, which is really confusing. I laugh to cover my embarrassment, then I notice I sit taller again. It all flows out. "I look at porn every day. I mean there are some days when I don't, but there are some days when I look at porn twice in the same day. And in the odd cases when I'm home alone all day and bored it could be even more than that."

"Does Anne Marie know?" she asks, getting curious.

"No, at least I don't think she does. I think I do a good job of hiding it. Mostly I look after she's gone to bed at night or if she's not home."

"How long has this been going on?"

"Since I got my first computer with an internet connection in college, so that's eighteen years. There have been periods when I didn't look at porn very much, but then there are times when I watch a lot, like multiple times a day."

"Interesting." There is no judgment in her tone. She is just shifting gears. "Well, I don't think you need to be embarrassed about it. It's a huge industry. I've coached so many men who look at porn. It's a huge part of the collective male consciousness on this planet. But it does steal your power and it exploits women, both of which aren't good."

"Yes, yes!" Her words, "it steals your power," resonate deeply with me. Occasionally, when Anne Marie and Maya were out of town, I'd gone on a porn-watching binge, and then felt tired and drained afterward. Like I had lost part of my life force. Then when I clawed my way back to reality the wave of guilt and shame would hit me, and I'd go back for more porn. There were days when I went back so many times that by the end of the day, I was just completely exhausted. No life force left. The only thing I could do was go to sleep.

The fact that she understands all of this comforts me. Suddenly I feel lighter, like a heavy weight is lifted off my shoulders.

"The good news is that I've coached this hundreds of times," she interrupts my thoughts. "You ready to get to work?"

"Yes." I sit up even straighter and close my eyes. *I am ready.* "Let's do it."

* * *

IT IS A FEW WEEKS after I came clean to Melissa about porn. I'm at the kitchen sink washing dishes when Anne Marie comes downstairs after putting Maya to bed. She picks up a towel, stands next to me, and starts drying a plate.

"So, how was your Melissa session today?" she asks.

"It was amazing." I stop what I'm doing and turn to look at her. "I haven't shared this with you yet, but a few weeks ago I told her that I watch porn more than I'd like, and that I feel like I need to stop."

Anne Marie clearly wasn't expecting this answer, and she looks at me with wide, surprised eyes. She puts down her towel and we take the conversation to the sofa, and I spend the next hour answering her questions. How long has this been going on? When do you do this? Where? How often?

I am an open book, and I share everything openly and honestly. She even asks what kinds of pornography I look at, which I also share, albeit sheepishly.

These are some of my most intimate secrets. Aside from my recent disclosures to Melissa, I haven't told *anyone* about this in my entire life, *ever*. I feel so exposed. But I also feel something completely unexpected: I feel liberated. And the conversation takes my relationship with Anne Marie to a completely new level. Sharing something this personal, this vulnerable—this is *true* intimacy. I'm not out of the woods yet, but I know I'm making progress.

Melissa is unrelenting. For several months we dive into the idea that I am weakening my power with porn. I begin to see that porn is a way of numbing or medicating myself, to avoid some kind of pain. We dig deep to try to understand that pain and where it might come from. Once again, my work with her is brutal, but also rewarding. I can feel myself opening up, almost like a flower starting to bloom.

I continue to be honest with Anne Marie about my habit and she is honest with me in return. The pornography bothers her, just like it did when I asked her to watch with me so many years ago in college. When she imagines me looking at other women's bodies, she feels violated, like I'm cheating on her. She finds it gross and repulsive. Fortunately, she also works with Melissa, who helps her process these things in the context of her own work.

I begin to track the number of days I go without looking at porn, and when I hit milestones, I am proud. I talk openly about it with my father. One time I even open up to Anne Marie's mom when we visit her in California.

"So, what's new with you?" she asks after we settle down at the table for dinner.

"Well, I look at porn more than I'd like, and I'm trying to break that habit," I say, matter-of-factly.

When Anne Marie and her mom almost spit out their food, I realize maybe I don't need to be *that* honest with everyone.

I continue working hard with Melissa, but after some initial progress I hit a wall. It turns out an eighteen-year porn habit is very hard to break. To try a different approach, she introduces a new concept of internal "identities." She tells me that we all have an entire population of identities that reside inside of us. We all have a "Hard Worker" identity, a "Partyer" identity, an "Honest Guy/Girl," a "Liar," an identity that cares about others, one that is selfish, etc. The list goes on and on. There are hundreds of them. All of us are all of these identities combined at the same time. Our personality that the world sees on the outside is the external expression of the identities inside of us that are most active or prominent.

Understanding this concept is powerful for me. It allows me to start viewing my porn habit with a bit more distance, almost like an observer. *Jason* is not looking at porn, one of his identities is. *Jason* is not a bad person, one of his identities is just acting out. Having this distance helps me feel less ashamed of myself and less embarrassed about my habit. This, in turn, allows me to study it more closely, with less internal judgment.

Of course, this identity of mine that liked to look at porn needed a name. "Let's call him Porn Star," Melissa says one day. We both laugh, and the name sticks.

* * *

MORE MONTHS PASS, AND I'M having another session with Melissa. Since giving a name to Porn Star, I've been gradually taking small steps toward getting to know him, to know my alter ego, the part of myself I've kept hidden in the shadows for much of my life. Not just in the shadows, in the dark. Some of my walls have started crumbling as I excavate parts of my foundation that have cracks. It's hard and painful work, but the more open I become with Melissa and Anne Marie, the lighter I feel. I am proud of myself for the work I am doing. And as I move through my days, I feel more alive. More mature. I am facing this thing that I've been so ashamed of and working to clean it up.

As my life comes into clearer focus, I realize that, at worst, my philandering will lead to the loss of my family and the loss of my career, and at best it will weaken my power and sabotage my efforts at building our venture capital firm. None of these things feels good, and I become even more intent on finally changing my behavior. I am not ready to tell anyone about my philandering, but I assure myself that if I stop the porn, the other stuff will stop too.

Melissa starts every session with the same question now: "So how is Porn Star this week?!" She is excited when she asks, like she can't wait to get caught up with the latest gossip or a favor-ite soap opera. Her levity helps break the seriousness and sets a non-judgmental tone for our calls, and I find myself sharing details that are so embarrassing that many times I can't even believe I'm saying them out loud.

The more I get to know Porn Star, the more I realize I don't like him. Correction: I *hate* him. Porn Star is sabotaging me. Porn

Star is loud. Porn Star is obnoxious. All he wants is money, women, and attention, and it becomes clear he will never have enough of these things. He also does not take any responsibility for his actions. He doesn't care that his behavior is putting the things I love and care about—my family and my career—at risk. Or that he is hurting innocent people along the way. He is a selfish asshole.

In today's session with Melissa, my eyes are closed as she guides me through envisioning all of my identities in a room together. It is an auditorium, and they are sitting in the seats, everyone except for one: Porn Star. He is on stage acting out and demanding everyone else's attention. My other identities grow annoyed with him. From the audience one of them yells, "Sit down and shut up, we are tired of you needing so much attention."

Porn Star stops in his tracks; the auditorium is silent while he glares back at the crowd.

"Fuck you!" he finally yells back. "Fuck you all. Without me you guys wouldn't have half the shit you have. That fancy house you're building? You wouldn't have that. Your fancy car? You wouldn't have that. You wouldn't have anything in your fancy life without me. You guys need me. You don't want to admit it, but I'm the guy who is making all of this shit happen while you just sit back and enjoy the money I bring in."

The auditorium is quiet for a while, and I am quiet on the phone. In that moment I realize that Porn Star is right. I hate him, but I *love* the lifestyle he has created for me. I hate him, but I *love* the freedom and power I have enjoyed from my wealth and fancy titles. I love the big house we are building. I love my flashy sports car. I love getting the women.

I begin to see that Porn Star has been a very important part of my life. He is the risk-taker. He is the schemer. He is the deal-maker. Without him, my life would be much, much different. I realize that by enjoying the fruits of Porn Star's actions, and even egging him on, I have been just as guilty as he was. Even worse, I have accused him of not taking responsibility when, really, *I* am the one who isn't taking responsibility.

In this world of internal identities, there needs to be a leader who takes responsibility for the entire population. I learn that I am that leader in my own internal world. As the leader, I have allowed Porn Star to play his games. I've done more than allow it, I have encouraged him in his exploits so that I could enjoy the results. If Porn Star is acting out, it is my fault. I need to start accepting responsibility for his actions. I need to start being a leader to my identities. Melissa helps guide me through all of these realizations and also helps me summarize them in the end.

"You need to grow up and be a leader." There is no criticism when she says this. It is merely a statement of fact.

The truth and simplicity of her words lands immediately, and with so much force that I am momentarily speechless.

"Yes, I need to grow up," I repeat. *It is time for me to grow up. But how?*

CHAPTER 11

"As children we are afraid of the dark.
As adults we are afraid of the light."

—DANY WATTS

FEBRUARY 2015

IT HAS BEEN EIGHT MONTHS SINCE I FIRST TOLD MELISSA about my porn habit. I am still proud of the work I'm doing and the progress I'm making. I am more honest; I live with more wisdom and consciousness. However, I had started from such a low point that I was still just getting started. To put it in terms of living with awareness, I was still relatively asleep. Fortunately, the universe has a way of sending us bigger and bigger wake-up calls until we get the message. And if it was looking for another wake-up call to send me, it didn't have to look far.

I noticed Lisa, the receptionist at the gym, the moment I'd stepped through the door the prior summer. She was young, in her mid-twenties, with a bubbly personality. Tall and lean, yet curvaceous at the same time, she checked off every box Porn Star scanned for.

I promised myself I would be on my best behavior. Those days were behind me.

It's almost funny for me to look back and think I had any power over what I was doing. The forces driving me were still too strong. Only it's not funny. Not at all. I white-knuckled, resisting for three full months, and while the days ticked by agonizingly slowly, I was proud of myself. I could control myself after all.

Until I couldn't.

Like a moth drawn to a flame, over the course of those three months our hellos and goodbyes kept getting longer and longer. In October I broke the barrier of professionalism by replying to one of her marketing emails with a cheeky response. When she replied with a smiley face, an electric charge ripped through my body. She knew what was up. The door was open. The game was on.

By the end of that month, we'd exchanged phone numbers and were texting short messages. Weeks later, I couldn't stop obsessing about what it would be like to be with her, and I began scheming ways that we could be alone together. And then, in the peak of my planning, something snapped. I don't recall what happened, but somehow, I had a moment of clarity that told me *You really don't want to do this. Stop now.*

In December, I canceled my gym membership. I knew I was getting pulled in, and I was determined to fight it. That moment would be akin to a drug addict getting rid of every bag of drugs they've hidden anywhere in their home, office, or car. Remove the drug, and you've removed the problem.

Except every addict knows it doesn't work that way.

My needs—for attention, or distraction, or to escape—persisted and remained strong. They pressed and they pressed. Eventually, I couldn't contain them any longer. After a month or so of no contact, we started texting again, this time with renewed vigor. I gave up on even trying to hold myself back, and she responded by leaning in even more.

We reached the point where we both plotted ways to be alone together. She lived with her mother so it was challenging to find times when she could disguise her whereabouts. Finally, one night we met in a parking lot near her home. It was the first time we were alone together outside the gym, and my body buzzed when she climbed into my car. It was a short rendezvous—all she had time for—and it left me wanting more. Much more.

As I drove home from the experience, whatever progress I had made in my coaching work seemed to have evaporated. Gone. I went right back to where I'd been years earlier, blindly following animal instincts with no thought of consequences and no regard for who I might be hurting in the process. I was focused on one thing, and one thing only: being alone with Lisa. It had to happen.

Looking at my calendar the next day I noticed that in a few weeks Anne Marie and Maya were leaving town to visit Anne Marie's parents for a long weekend. I would be home alone for four days. *Perfect.* I solidified plans with Lisa to meet at a hotel the night after Anne Marie and Maya were set to leave.

The entire encounter was nothing like what I fantasized it would be. I was anxious the whole time. Something wasn't right. I drove home feeling hollow, but by this point, that wasn't anything new. I almost always went home from these experiences feeling hollow.

The uneasy feeling was still with me at home, and I climbed into bed feeling sad and lonely and lost, feelings I hadn't felt in quite a long time by now. But here I was again. I had failed myself, *again*. I had so many positive things in my life, and yet I had just wasted an entire evening in the pursuit of some kind of thrill that would put my marriage at risk, *and* which hadn't even satiated me for more than a few minutes. Eventually I drifted off to a night of restless sleep.

The next morning my phone rang early. Too early. It was the woman with the raspy voice.

"Where is my daughter?"

* * *

AFTER I DROP MY PARENTS off at their timeshare to rest for the afternoon, I return to my home to speak with Melissa. I explain everything, and the conversation turns toward what should happen next.

"You know you have to tell Anne Marie," she says.

I hang my head. "Yes, I know."

"When are you going to tell her?"

"I guess when she gets home."

"No, no. I don't think that's a good idea. I think it's better for you to tell her while she's still with her parents. She's going to need them."

Need her parents? Is this really that serious?

Yes, yes it is.

"Okay." I grimace just thinking about it. "That's going to be really hard." Blowing out a breath, I have an idea. "Are you available to talk on the phone with us?"

"Yes, I can do that this evening."

We spend a few minutes rehearsing what I'm going to say, and then she reassures me that she is going to help us through this.

"I have a feeling something big is about to get unlocked," she ends our call.

A few hours later I drop my parents off at a pottery-making place so they can go in and get situated for our upcoming class. I tell them I have a quick call to make for work and that I'll be in as soon as I can.

I had exchanged texts with Anne Marie earlier to arrange a time for us to talk. When we get on the phone, I don't waste any time. A similar conversation happened almost one year ago, and I know it will be best if I just get right to the point.

"I did something I shouldn't have, and I want to tell you about it, and I'd like Melissa to be on the phone when I tell you."

"Okay." Her voice sounds unsettled.

I conference Melissa in. When she gets on the phone, I come out with the story. I tell the whole truth, much the way I had rehearsed it, not trying to spin or cover anything up for a change. Anne Marie was silent the entire time.

When I finish, Melissa asks Anne Marie if she is okay.

"No." It's clear she's crying.

Melissa takes over. "Jason, I'm going to talk with Anne Marie privately now."

"Yes, of course.

"I'll call you when we're done."

"Okay." Then, before I let them go, I add, "I'm really sorry about this, Anne Marie."

I sit in the car, in the dark. My mom comes out to check on me. "We are about to start," she says, then seems to notice something isn't right. "Is everything okay?"

"Yes and no," I tell her. "I'm sorry, but this conversation is going to take longer than I thought. They are calling me back in a few minutes. I'll just come in when I can."

She nods and goes back inside.

I stare out the windshield. My mind is blank. Once more I'm numb. About twenty minutes later my phone rings. It is Melissa.

"She's really hurt, Jason."

"Yeah, I'm sure."

"She needs to go home tomorrow because of work on Monday, but she doesn't want you or your parents to be around."

"Okay."

"Can you guys go somewhere? Maybe get a hotel?"

"Yes, we can do that."

"Okay, good." I hear her sigh. "I'm not going to lie, Jason, this isn't good."

"I know."

"Let's talk again tomorrow afternoon."

After we hang up, I sit in the car in silence for a few more minutes, my heart aching for Anne Marie. She is a strong soul, but even the sturdiest among us have their limits. *I've gone too far this time. I've finally destroyed my marriage, the thing I care the most about. What have I done?*

Eventually I get out and go into the pottery-making place to find my parents. Their faces are beaming with pride as they tell me how much fun they had and show me their creations. But I must look like I've seen a ghost because their excitement quickly turns to concern.

"You okay, bud?" Bill asks.

"No. Not really. I'll tell you about it when we get in the car."

And so I do. Sitting in the parking lot in my car, I tell them an abridged version of the story, starting with the usual "I did something I shouldn't have..." and including just enough details to get the point across. I'm so embarrassed. They listen quietly. I finish by telling them that, even though our plans have the three of us flying to San Francisco three days later, we are going to leave town tomorrow and stay in a hotel in Salt Lake City for two nights.

"Anne Marie has to come home to work, and she doesn't want us to be around when she arrives."

"I don't blame her," Mom says. There is sadness in her voice.

The three of us don't speak for a full minute while the gravity of the situation sinks in. Eventually, my mom breaks the silence. "Why did you do that, J?"

I look through the windshield out into the darkness and shake my head. "I don't know, Mom. I don't know."

* * *

THE NEXT DAY WE PACK up our things, leave the house, and check into a hotel in Salt Lake City. It is cold, and there isn't much to do, so I spend a lot of time sitting in my room thinking about what is happening. Occasionally, I'll walk around the block a few times for fresh air. I have a conversation that afternoon with Melissa and learn she talked to Anne Marie again that morning.

Melissa tells me Anne Marie is, understandably, really upset and very hurt. For me to do something like this *twice*, after everything she and I have been through, is just unbelievable to her...as in literally hard to believe that it is actually happening. She is starting to feel like she doesn't even know who I am. She doesn't want to see me, and she doesn't want to talk to me. She needs time to think.

"And neither of us believe you that this was an isolated event," Melissa finishes.

I am mostly quiet as I listen, pacing around my hotel room. I am nervous and scared about where this is heading.

"Jason," Melissa prods. "Are you *sure* you haven't done this sort of thing before?"

I stop pacing. *I don't have to tell her. I can keep my secrets buried.* I am silent.

After a long quiet moment, she continues; this time her voice sounds soft, almost sad. "Jason, if you don't tell the truth, you will never get well."

I know she is right. My life is unraveling right in front of my eyes. What else needs to happen to me before I will finally stop running? Stop hiding? Stop pretending? Through her, the universe is whispering to me now. *Wake up, Jason. Wake up. Wake up.*

Was I finally ready to listen? What will happen if I tell the truth?

I sit down on the edge of the bed, close my eyes, and hang my head. I see a vision of myself on a tall cliff. I want to take the next step, but there is nothing to put my foot on. If I step, I will tumble off into a black abyss. There is no bottom that I can see. I will just keep falling. Falling into nothingness. Falling into an uncertain future. A future I can't control.

In my vision I look over my shoulder and all the porn, all the women, are coming toward me. The only way to get away from them is to step off the cliff. To have faith. Faith that whatever happens in that uncertain future will be better than staying in the dark. I might lose Anne Marie. I might lose Maya. But I can see now that it is the only way out. I need to be brave. I need to have courage. I need to take that step.

"No." I feel so weak, it is all I can muster.

My foot extends over the side of the cliff.

"No, what?"

"No, this isn't the only time."

I am shifting my weight forward.

"Okay. How many times has this happened?"

"I don't know." I close my eyes tighter and shake my head. "Too many to count."

I'm falling now.

"How long ago did this start?"

"It's been happening as far back as I can remember."

"Like, before you and Anne Marie separated?"

"Yes. It started way before that."

Falling...

"Oh, wow." She doesn't say it with surprise, more like a recognition that a big wound is about to get exposed. "You poor thing. You've been keeping these secrets for a long time."

"Yeah." Tears trickle down my cheeks.

"Secrets will keep you sick, Jason."

"Yeah, I know."

"Do you have a notebook with you?"

"Yes, I do."

"I want you to go back to the beginning and write down every instance you can remember. Can you do that?"

The earth continues opening up under me, and I continue falling.

"Yes, I can do that."

"Don't worry about what's going to happen with Anne Marie. I'll talk to her. You just need to focus on getting well, okay?"

"Okay."

"I'll check in with you tomorrow."

I stay sitting on the edge of the bed for a long time after that. I have walked off the cliff. I am falling into the abyss.

Eventually my awareness returns, and I go to my bag, get my notebook and a pen, and sit on the bed. It is the notebook where I keep notes and to-do lists for work. I skip to a blank page near the back and stare at it for a while.

Melissa said to go back to the beginning, so that's where I start. I write the first entry slowly.

"Living in Mt. View. AMP in LA. Before engagement. Craigslist. Sex."

I stare at the entry for a minute. Then the next one comes to me.

"Another Craigslist. Had a beer then went back to my apartment. Sex."

And it continues. At first the experiences come back slowly and in chronological order. Each one is like a small movie I can play in my head. But then it all just starts flooding into me faster and faster. Random images start flashing through my mind. Wallpapered hotel hallways. Naked bodies on beds. White envelopes filled with money. Online pictures of women in lingerie. I can't write fast enough to keep up. I have to close my eyes and take deep breaths every few minutes to focus again.

At some point I notice it is dark outside, and my hand is cramping. I don't know how long I've been writing, but I have only just scratched the surface. I force myself to take a break. I get up, take a shower, and then take my notebook to the desk in my hotel room, turn on the lamp, and continue writing. I write several more pages, until my hand starts cramping again, and then turn off the light and climb into bed. My mind is dull and exhausted, and I fall asleep quickly.

It is still dark outside when I wake the next morning. I immediately go to the desk, turn on the light, and start writing again. This time things move slower, and I write the stories with much more detail. Another woman from Craigslist. Another woman from SeekingArrangement. A Hampton Inn. A parking garage. A massage parlor. I write a detailed account of the encounter with Leslie, from the portfolio company, in her apartment. As I write it, I realize I still have her number in my phone, and so I get my phone and delete her contact card.

I write about the time a year or two ago, while I was in San Francisco for work, that I called one of the women I dated back in 2010 when Anne Marie and I were separated and invited her to spend the night with me. I knew she was married by then and living in the suburbs with her husband, but that didn't deter me. I wrote about how angry she got, and how much it stung when she said, "I thought you were different. Now I realize you're just like every other guy. Don't call me again." As I write the story, I realize I still have her contact information in my phone too, so I pick up my phone and delete it.

I write, and I write, and I write. There are so many stories. Too many. Eventually I take a break to get breakfast with my parents at the McDonald's across the street. I tell them about my conversation with Melissa the day before, and that I am doing some intensive journaling.

"Take whatever time you need," my mom says.

Back in my room I start writing more details about my experiences building profiles on websites over the years. As I write about it, I remember I still have pictures of myself on my computer that I used for my profiles, never with my face in them, and often without a shirt on. I delete all the pictures. While I am doing that, I start searching around old folders where I've stashed porn images and videos and delete any that I find.

This pattern continues for a while longer. Eventually I take a break to have lunch, then walk around the block by myself for fresh air before heading back to my room for another call with Melissa.

"How's it going today?" she asks.

"I've been writing and writing, and it feels good to let it all out."

"Yeah, I'm sure it does."

I tell her about what I've written. Not every detail, just that there are so many stories and so many secrets. I tell her about deleting my stashes of porn. I tell her that at some point about a year ago I realized I had a serious problem, but I didn't know what to do about it, and no matter how hard I'd tried over the years I couldn't seem to stop myself.

"Have you considered one of the twelve step programs?" she asks.

"You mean like Alcoholics Anonymous? No, I hadn't considered that. Why?"

"Well, there is one for sex addiction. Maybe you can see if there are meetings for that in your area."

Sex addiction? Wait. I know I have a problem, but am I an addict?

"You really think that would help?"

"I don't know, but isn't it worth a try?"

I stare out the window. Everything that seemed so solid in my life a few days ago now seems completely shattered. The only thing that is certain now is that there is no turning back.

"Yeah, I guess so," I say. "I'll try anything right now. I don't want to lose Anne Marie and Maya."

"I'm talking to Anne Marie in a little while. I think she should know about all of this history. Do I have your permission to share this with her?"

I lean my head against the windowpane.

"Yes, sure." Tears well up again. "Please tell her I'm really sorry, and I'm going to be completely honest, and I'm really serious about getting help."

"I will. And don't worry, there are going to be lessons in this for her too."

"Okay."

"Let's check in again tomorrow. In the meantime, just keep writing."

* * *

THAT EVENING I KEEP WRITING. It is a mixture of recording past stories and capturing how I'm feeling that moment. I have never journaled before, and it feels good to write down my thoughts and feelings. Eventually I realize that I feel dirty, so I stop writing and go take a shower.

While I'm in the shower I remember that I'm supposed to look up twelve-step programs. I dry off and brush my teeth, then take my laptop to my desk and open it up. I have some awareness that sitting in front of my laptop after washing up for bed is a familiar experience. For nineteen years—fully half of my life—the computer screen has been a portal to a dark, underground world that I typically accessed alone and at night. There was porn. Sex. Secrets. But this time I'm not going to use my computer to go into the dark. This is different now.

I Google search "twelve step program for sex," and I'm surprised at the results. There are so many links for porn addiction and sex addiction. I click on a few and start reading.

"Sex addiction encompasses everything from heavy pornography consumption to promiscuity."[1]

I swallow hard. *Yes, I engage in both of those.*

I keep reading.

"We admitted we were powerless over addictive sexual behavior—that our lives had become unmanageable."[2]

I close my eyes. *This sounds like my life. Yes, I guess I am an addict. How did this happen to me?*

---

[1] https://www.recovery.org/support-groups/sexaholics-anonymous/

[2] https://saa-recovery.org/our-program/the-twelve-steps/

I force my eyes open and keep reading.

Eventually I click and read my way to a page for Sexaholics Anonymous, and once there, I am hooked. I absorb every word. It all resonates deep in my heart. Deep in my soul. I am both amazed and shocked at how accurately it describes my life. I have tried to stop myself so many times, but couldn't. My behavior had continued to escalate and was becoming more reckless and more dangerous, both to myself and to the people I loved. I am at risk of losing the things in my life that mean the most to me.

I click on a link to find a meeting near me, and once again I am surprised at the results. There are dozens of meetings in Salt Lake City. There are meetings every day of the week. The idea that there are groups of people gathering to talk about sex addiction in so many places, and so frequently, takes me completely by surprise. *Is this really that common of a thing? Are there really this many people struggling with the same thing I am?* Over the next several weeks I will learn that the answers to those questions are a resounding "Yes and Yes."

I have to go to San Francisco with my parents the following day, but it will be a quick trip, and I'll be back a few days later. I find a meeting that works for my schedule, and then send Melissa an email letting her know I'll be attending my first Sexaholics Anonymous meeting.

I close my laptop, crawl into bed, and lay still, staring at the ceiling. My mind is so quiet I have a sensation that time is slowing down. For decades I have been racing and racing. Running and running. First, I was running from my feelings. Then I was running from my secrets. Looking for places to hide. I had tried to slow down, but something always made me start running again. Was this time going to be different? *Yes. It is.* Already, something about this time feels different.

Yesterday I was falling into an abyss. But now I realize I'm not falling anymore. I feel wobbly and unsure of my footing, but I'm standing. I turned my back on the dark and stepped off the ledge, and I'm okay. I'm still here.

My mind drifts to Anne Marie. I still don't want to lose her, but I start to realize that I have to let go of that fear. Fear of losing her prevented me from being honest five years ago, when her secrets came out. I kept my secrets inside because I was afraid that if I revealed them, she would stop loving me. Instead of being honest, I wanted her to love a me that wasn't real. Instead of working on myself *for* myself, I had worked on myself for *her*. I had only scratched the surface because I wasn't really doing the work to get myself well, I was doing the work to avoid losing her. She is doing her work, and she is standing on her own two feet now. When will I start standing on *my* own two feet?

Now. Now. This is where I will make my stand.

Melissa talked to me about not keeping secrets five years ago, in my very first session, and in so many sessions since then. "The truth speeds everything up," she would say. "The truth will set you free." Countless times I heard the words, but I never really understood what she meant. Now, alone in this hotel room, laying next to a notebook full of confessions, I feel it. *Now* I understand. If I don't get my secrets out, they will keep destroying me from the inside out. They will take away everything I care about, and I will be stuck in the dark, forever. My secrets have to come out. I *want* them to come out. If Anne Marie isn't going to love me because I show her the real me, that is a chance I have to take. I have to start being the real me. I have to start being honest.

Once again, I have a feeling like everything that was important to me before—the money, the cars, the women—isn't anymore. The only thing that is important is getting well. My body shivers as these feelings pass through me. Already I am feeling the early stages of the liberation that comes from telling the truth. And then I think of the Sexaholics Anonymous website. The list of meeting times. Every line on that list is a group of people who have found the courage to tell the truth. I want to be like them. I want to be brave. Another feeling moves through me. *I'm not alone anymore.*

* * *

TWO DAYS LATER, WHILE I'M in San Francisco, Anne Marie and I have a joint call with Melissa. It is the first time I've been on the phone with her since the night the news broke. It is a very uncomfortable conversation, and we are lucky to have Melissa there to referee. We've each been talking to her for five years at this point. She knows each of us better than anyone else on the planet, and we have both grown to trust her.

After a brief intro by Melissa to set the stage, Anne Marie starts in with her questions. She is angry, and they are rapid-fire.

When were you doing this? With who? How did you meet these women? Where did these things happen?

I answer her questions honestly. Eventually her anger gives way to her pain underneath, and she starts crying. I blubber apologies, and then Melissa steps in to buoy us both.

By the end of the conversation the rules of engagement have been set and agreed. The message to me from both Melissa and Anne Marie is clear: I need to grow up, and I need to do it fast. Anne Marie's patience is razor thin, and if I don't show signs that I am taking this deadly seriously, she will leave me. I also need to find a place to live. Anne Marie doesn't want me back in our rental house.

"For how long?" I ask, somewhat naively.

Anne Marie replies simply: "I don't know."

"What will we tell Maya?"

"Melissa and I talked about that. We'll tell her you're working on a big project, which is the truth."

"Okay." So much of this was out of my hands now.

Melissa turns her attention to Anne Marie, and I am a bit surprised at how intense the message is for her as well. We'd both learned over the years that we aren't victims—that we create everything that happens to us in our lives for a reason, even if that reason is difficult to see in the moment. Melissa reminds Anne Marie that if she was co-creating with me for so long while this was all going on in the background, she must have been getting some benefit out of it too. She was going to have to dig deep to understand, and take responsibility for, her side of it.

Before we all get off the phone, Anne Marie has something else to say.

"I want to know all of the details."

I take a minute to digest her request.

"I can read you what I've written in my journal. I'm not keeping secrets anymore."

Melissa jumps in. "That's fine, Anne Marie, but be careful. It could be counterproductive."

Anne Marie was clear. "I don't care about that right now."

"When do you want to have that conversation?" I ask.

There is ice in her voice now. "Anytime. Right after this call is fine."

We all talk a bit longer and then Melissa drops off the call, leaving Anne Marie and I alone on the phone for the first time since this whole thing blew open.

"I'm really sorry, Anne Marie." I start. "I think I have a problem. I fly back to Utah tomorrow and I'm going to a Sexaholics Anonymous meeting the next day."

"I know, Melissa told me."

She has no interest in having a conversation. She just wants to know the details.

"Where do you want me to start?" I ask.

"At the beginning."

"Okay..."

...and so I proceed to start reading my journal entries to her over the phone. She interrupts me with periodic questions, which I answer honestly, assuming I can remember the details she is asking for. There is one question she keeps asking that I can never answer, though.

"What was her name?" she asks after I finish reading the first entry.

"I don't remember."

That infuriates her. *"You don't remember?"*

"No, I swear. I don't remember."

"Okay. Continue."

Then another entry. Then the question again.

"What was *her* name?"

I pinch the bridge of my nose, trying to remember email or text exchanges where I might have seen a name, but it was all blank. "I don't remember," I finally say, slumping further in my chair.

"Seriously?!" Now she sounds angrier than I've ever heard her.

"Yeah, I'm serious."

Then another. Then another.

It hadn't occurred to me when I was journaling, but now it was glaringly obvious. I flip several pages ahead in my journal, scanning every entry. The only ones that have names are women I dated when we were separated. I'd written no names for any of the women I'd met through Craigslist or escort sites or SeekingArrangement. I stare at the pages in disbelief. I can't remember any of their names. The reality of this hits me hard.

I stop reading and just say, "I'm so sorry, Anne Marie. I have a serious problem."

"Yeah, you do. And you need to fix it."

"I will. I will. I promise you, I will."

The next morning, I write this journal entry:

"Read all of that to Anne Marie yesterday. It was hard on her. I felt really bad. It is so clear that I was (am) very sick. It had nothing to do with her."

CHAPTER 12

"During the dark night there is no choice but to surrender control, give in to unknowing, and stop and listen to whatever signals of wisdom might come along. It's a time of enforced retreat and perhaps unwilling withdrawal. The dark night is more than a learning experience; it's a profound initiation into a realm that nothing in the culture, so preoccupied with external concerns and material success, prepares you for."

—THOMAS MOORE, *Dark Nights of the Soul*

FEBRUARY 2015

IT IS JUST AFTER SEVEN O'CLOCK ON A FRIDAY EVENING. I am seated in a folding-chair circle with at least thirty strangers. I hold my breath. My body tenses. My turn is next, and I'm terrified.

The person to my right stops talking, and the room goes silent. Everyone is looking at me. My eyes are open, but I can't see anything.

"Hi, my name is Jason, and I'm a sexaholic."

Dislodging the words from my throat is so hard that they come out almost a mumble. But as my eyes regain focus, I see everyone in the circle nodding. They know it's hard. They remember their first meeting too.

I watch as the rest of the circle continues to introduce themselves. For the next hour I am transported into a different world. A world where people freely admit that they are imperfect. That they are struggling. We all landed here because our lives had become unmanageable. At some point we surrendered to the fact that we were powerless to change, and that we needed help.

I am surprised by the diversity of the group. Men and women. Young and old. All different backgrounds. I'm still too embarrassed to share my story, but I listen intently as others share theirs. Some have been sexually sober for one day. Others are celebrating years and even decades of sobriety. I am inspired by their stories, but not always for the same reasons.

Some of them tell stories of overcoming significant obstacles, or repairing broken lives, and how their lives only changed once they started "working the steps." These stories inspire me because that is what I want for my future. Conversely, some of the stories paint vivid images of lives that had spiraled out of control and brought significant pain to the individual and the people they loved. Divorce. Financial hardship. Estrangement from children. Broken careers. Negative health consequences. These stories show me what my life is trending toward if I don't do something to change. I am already hurting the people I love and taking greater risks with my career, my health, and my safety. If I don't change, I can easily wind up heading down the same path they had.

Everyone is honest, and my unwillingness to share my story tells me how brave they are for sharing theirs. These are the bravest and most honest people I've ever been with. I suddenly feel a longing to become part of this new family.

One of the men volunteers to speak with new attendees after the meeting, so when the meeting ends, I seek him out. He shakes my hand and says, "I'm glad you're here." His four simple words pierce straight into my heart. I have felt lost and alone and scared for so long. Lying and pretending and hiding behind a façade. With those four words he tells me that I don't have to pretend anymore. I am welcome here, just as I am. The real me. I belong.

He makes sure I get all the literature, and then offers some parting advice. "Try a lot of different meetings until you find a day and time and group that really speaks to you."

* * *

IT IS ONE WEEK LATER. I sit on the stairs in a one-bedroom loft apartment and stare into the efficiency kitchen. I try to force myself to eat a bowl of cereal, but my stomach is so twisted up in knots that I can't eat. The small apartment is where I will live for...I don't know how long. Anne Marie doesn't want to see me, and she doesn't want me to be around Maya. I have canceled all my business calls and trips. I have no secret rendezvous to coordinate. I have nothing I'm supposed to do in this moment but eat my cereal. There is nothing to distract me from sitting in the vacuum of stillness and mess that is now my life. The silence of the room mirrors the silence in my head. It is deafening.

After the initial shock of my revelation, and the early hope I felt as I started sharing my secrets, the reality—and gravity—of my situation sinks in. Consequently, my mood drops as my hopes are dashed. Very quickly, I go from riding high, lost in the excitement of the chase, to watching my life crash down around me. I've been kicked out of my house. Anne Marie is probably going to divorce me, which will also mean missing out on a big part of Maya's life. Twice in the last week I woke up soaked with sweat from a nightmare that the woman with the raspy voice was chasing me. She haunts me in the daytime too. Several times my mind flashes images of her doing something to publicly expose what I'd done, which would be very embarrassing for me and, more importantly, for Anne Marie.

I tell my parents what is happening. Anne Marie tells her parents. I can't hide the way it is disrupting my work, so I have to tell my closest business associates. The embarrassments mount. I want to run and hide more than ever, but I also know I can't do that anymore.

Yesterday Melissa forwarded me an article she remembered reading just over a year ago, about a Google executive who died on his yacht while doing drugs with a woman he met on SeekingArrangement.

"That's scary, Jason," she said, and she was right. That was my future. That was the path I was heading down. If I don't change, I will eventually self-destruct somehow. But I have tried to change so many times, and I failed every time. There are moments when I'm convinced that this time is different, that I really am going to change now that I'm telling all my secrets. But those moments are fleeting. Mostly I am afraid this time will be no different. I will wind up right back in the same place. Back on the same path. Back in the dark.

My gaze drops to the floor as I think about the last several nights. As I lay in bed, feelings of shame, embarrassment, failure, and fear crawl over my skin. When I finally fall asleep, I toss and turn deep into the nights. Between that and the nightmare returning, I've barely slept, and the sleep deprivation is only adding to my sense of confusion. I have no idea what I'm supposed to do with myself. I am completely lost. I know I can't continue to be the guy I've been for twenty years, but I don't know who I'm supposed to become. I know I can't continue to live the way I have been, but I have no idea what it feels like to live any other way. Who am I supposed to be? How am I supposed to live?

I am aimless. Aimless and in constant struggle to maintain my sobriety, which seems almost more than I can bear.

Looking up again, my eye notices a book on the kitchen counter, *The Twelve Steps of Sexaholics Anonymous*, and I remember something I heard in my first meeting: I don't have to know what to do, I just have to follow the steps. I just have to go to a meeting. I just have to put one foot in front of the other. The realization wakes me up a little, and I sit up straighter and take in the room again. Back in the moment, I'm able to get up and start moving.

Over the next two weeks, Sexaholics Anonymous (SA) becomes my savior. I attend at least one SA meeting every day, usually two. Some are during the day; some are in the evening. Some are in nondescript office buildings; others are in churches. I find a few meetings I like best and eventually settle into a routine of attending two to three meetings a week. I also voraciously consume the SA literature. Going to meetings and reading the books gives me clarity and direction as I sit in my identity crisis, but I still experience violent emotional swings as part of my struggle to stay sober.

According to SA, to count days of sexual sobriety I have to abstain from all manner of sexual activity, including pornography, masturbation, and sexual fantasies/lusting. Sex with my spouse is acceptable, but given the circumstances, that is not an option. My days-of-sobriety count is the only ruler I have to measure whether I am succeeding in my recovery or not. Failing at recovery would almost certainly mean divorce and the loss of my family. And it would probably mean continuing deeper into my downward spiral, eventually to some point of no return. My sobriety day count takes on incredible significance to me.

I have been masturbating, usually to pornography, almost every day for close to twenty years. I am completely addicted to it, to the temporary peace I experience when I disappear alone with my fantasies, and the numbness I feel after orgasm. If the urge to look at porn or fantasize about sex surfaces, I am supposed to breathe and let the feeling move through me. Or journal about it. Or call my SA sponsor. Or go for a walk. Or do all of these things. Anything to keep my balance. Anything to avoid acting out the urge.

This is excruciatingly difficult for me to do. When urges arrive, time stands still. Seconds feel like hours. Minutes feel like days. When I successfully string together a series of sober days, I am so proud of myself and so excited about my progress that I border on euphoria. I journal about how well I am doing. How excited I am about my new life. How I finally feel at peace. I call Anne Marie and share my news, eager to show her how much I am changing, and how quickly.

But often, the bulb that burns twice as bright burns half as long. Inevitably, within a matter of days, a wave hits me that is so big I am powerless to stop it. As my sobriety day count drops back to zero, my hopes drop even lower. My journal entries on these days reflect my feelings of despair. Drowning in the terror of an unknown future, I write frantically about how I will never be able to change. How I am doomed to fail, and everything dear to me will be taken away. I avoid talking to Anne Marie for a day or two, but eventually we talk, and she asks how it's going, and I can feel her disappointment when I tell her. The third time this happens she doesn't say much on the phone, and I feel her start slipping further away from me, which scares me even more.

I remember lying in bed alone in the hotel in Salt Lake City the day everything changed, and realizing I had to let go of the fear of losing Anne Marie if I wanted to get well. *Actually* letting go was turning out to be much harder to do. But I was still flailing around trying to find my balance, and if I stayed connected to her, I would drag her down with me. She was so hurt, and she needed to focus on her own version of recovering from the recent trauma. Eventually, the frequency of our calls lessens, and I stop sharing details of what I am going through. Both of these changes only increase my feelings of fear and isolation.

One night when I am in my apartment, I go to bed particularly frightened. I have been sober for a record six days. It feels like six years. I am afraid I won't be able to hold out much longer, and I know the middle of the night is when the worst urges will arrive. A long night, lying alone in bed, can feel like an eternity. I am afraid. I am afraid to change, and I am afraid to stay the same. I am afraid of the shame I will feel when I inevitably act out.

I awake from a restless sleep in the middle of the night, and the urge is just too strong. I can't stop myself. Afterward I drift off to another restless sleep. Sometime later, still in the middle of the night, I wake up feeling completely lost, and gripped by the most intense fear I've ever felt. *Who am I? What am I doing? What is going to happen to me?*

Half asleep and somewhat mechanically, I make my way over to the window of my bedroom and look out. I left it open for cool air, and there is only a thin screen separating me from the night. I am at least five stories above the back patio. For a fraction of a second a thought floats through my head: *If I fall, this will all be over. I won't have to be so afraid anymore.*

I've never had a thought like that in my life, and it scares the shit out of me. As I regain my senses, I am so afraid of the window that I lock it and move a chair in front of it to block my access. I get back in bed and stare at the ceiling. *Is this nightmare ever going to end?*

The experience at the window that night is a turning point. The idea that feeling nothing would be better than feeling scared activated something inside me. I had been running away from my feelings for my entire life, and look where it had gotten me. Maybe I needed to stop avoiding my feelings.

I call one of my SA sponsors the next morning and tell him I am feeling disappointed with myself and scared that I will never be able to get sober. A soft-spoken man who has been sober for twenty-five years, he reassures me that what I'm going through is a normal part of my recovery process. In that call he helps me see that I'm putting the wrong emphasis on my sobriety day count.

"Your goal is not to have a high number," he says. "Your goal is to love yourself, to be humble and realize you can't do this alone, and to live a simple life with integrity. If you do those things, your day count will naturally rise. The count is not the goal; it is the result of striving for those other goals."

He is right. I am much too focused on my "number." The pride I feel when my number rises hits euphoric levels because I'm projecting a lifetime of recovery all in a single moment. Conversely, the despair I feel when my number falls is a projected lifetime of failure. Projecting my entire future, either of success or failure, creates so much pressure that it actually pushes me to act out.

"Don't put so much pressure on yourself," he tells me. "Don't focus on the future. Just focus on today."

Stay in the present moment. *Be* in the present moment. Melissa had told me this so many times. As had Eckhart Tolle in *The Power of Now*, a book I'd read a few years prior. And now I was finally hearing all of them at the same time. I didn't need to project a lifetime of success. Or a lifetime of failure. I didn't need to know who I was supposed to become or how I was supposed to live. I just had to know who I was right now, and how I was going to live today.

Today, I am an addict. Today, I will only do things that will help me in my addiction recovery. I will go to a meeting. I will read SA literature. I will be honest with myself about my addiction. I will journal about my addiction. I will talk with Melissa about it.

From that moment forward, everything I do, all day, every day, is focused on my recovery.

* * *

IT ISN'T EASY. AND NO matter how much work I do, the long nights alone continue to be the most difficult. After almost a full month of restless nights and nightmares, I can barely function. My head is in a perpetual fog.

Part of my recovery includes taking care of myself, and part of taking care of myself means I have to figure out a way to get some sleep. I already stopped drinking alcohol because I noticed that just one beer or glass of wine with dinner made it much more likely I would struggle with sexual urges at night. That helped a little, but it wasn't enough. I hadn't exercised at all since this whole thing started, and I suspect doing something physical will help me sleep. I have no interest in going to a gym though, so I decide to try something new: yoga.

I look online and find a late morning yoga class at a nearby studio, and the next morning I drive over in a heavy March snow-storm. A nice woman greets me at the front desk, takes my pay-ment, hands me a rented mat, and tells me to pick anyplace I like inside the studio, adding, "Class will start in about ten minutes."

I take off my snowy boots and enter the room. Immediately, I am enveloped by a fragrance of burning incense and candles that is so thick it makes the air feel like it has texture. There are small stone statues that look like Hindu deities lining the edges of the hardwood floor. I am the first one here, so I lay my mat down near the middle of the room, sit on it, and wait.

Eventually three women enter and sit on their mats. Then finally the nice woman from the front desk comes in, and she sits on her mat at the front of the room.

"Hi, I'm Stephanie," she says in a soothing voice. "Thank you for being here today."

She turns on soft music and asks us to close our eyes. "Take a breath and think of someone you want to dedicate your practice to this morning and hold that person in your mind for a moment." I see an image of Anne Marie, and I dedicate my practice to her. Then we begin.

I don't know the names of any of the poses, so I watch Stephanie the entire time to understand where I'm supposed to put my hands and feet. The other women seem to be moving easily, but I am so inflexible that my poses look nothing like theirs. I become self-conscious.

Stephanie must notice my discomfort because she gently tells the class, "Remember that yoga is like life. It is a personal journey. Focus on your journey. Focus on your breath."

I stop trying to effort my way in and out of the poses and start moving more slowly and breathing more deeply. Stephanie tells us that we can always rest in something called child's pose if we need to, and I spend at least half of that first class crouched on my knees, with my arms stretched in front of me, and my forehead resting on the mat.

Despite my difficulties, by the end of class I feel good, and that night I have the best night of sleep I've had in a month. I go back for another class a few days later and while I'm there I sign up for a membership, buy a mat, and take home a schedule. Before I know it, I'm going to yoga every day, usually twice a day, once in the morning and once at night. I dedicate my practices to Anne Marie or to Maya, and sometimes to myself if I'm having a rough day. It doesn't take me long to learn the basic poses and get a bit more flexible. And as I get more comfortable on my mat, and my body learns how to move in and out of the poses, my mind starts to get quieter. I don't have to think as much. I just move. And I breathe. And I hold a pose. And I breathe again.

Eventually, I am so focused on moving my body and holding my poses and feeling my breathing that I lose track of time. I lose track of everything. The only things I feel are my body and my breathing. I'm not scared. I'm not embarrassed. I'm not lost. I'm not confused.

Holding poses and breathing doesn't just quiet my mind and calm me down; it also gives me a new way to exist inside my body. Up until this point in my life, the relationship I had with my body was mostly mechanical. My body was a thing that was separate and apart from myself. My body's job was to carry around my head, which was where *I* lived. I gave my body fuel and I lifted weights to keep it strong, and then I expected it to do its job.

Through some alchemy I'm not sure I understand, yoga starts to change this. While holding poses and focusing on my breathing, parts of my awareness start to move into my body. I start to *embody* my body. I begin to notice the subtle sensations inside of it. My mind communicates with me in words, and that was a language I understood, so for decades I gave my mind all my attention. I start to understand that my body communicates with me in a language of feelings and sensations that I had almost entirely ignored before.

Because I'm listening to my body more carefully, I also notice that, similar to alcohol, when I eat meat, I'm more likely to have sexual urges at night and I don't sleep as well, so I shift to a pescatarian diet. Melissa reminds me to go back to some of the guided meditations she told me about years ago, and the combination of diet changes, yoga, and bedtime guided meditations helps me get back to restful nights of sleep.

* * *

IT IS TEN-THIRTY ON A Wednesday morning, and I have just begun a call with Melissa. While the twelve steps of SA provide a roadmap for me to repair my broken life and start heading down a new path, Melissa keeps her focus on helping me untangle completely from my old life. In recent sessions, we have spoken at length about the collective consciousness of our society and the gender stereotypes it encourages, and how I had fallen right into them. Somehow a lifetime of imagery from movies, television, and magazines, reinforced by interactions with men in my life or stories of high-profile men behaving badly, had taught me that my goals as a man were more money, more power, faster cars, and more women. And the collective promised me that if I had those things, I would be happy. So, I did what a lot of men do, and I went out and I got those things.

"Now," Melissa says, "if I put two boxes on a table, and one is filled with money, cars, and women, and the other is filled with Anne Marie and Maya, which box would you choose?"

"Well of course I would choose the box with Anne Marie and Maya." The answer comes to me easily. There is no question. It is no contest. "But if it is so clear and easy to see that now, why wasn't it clear before?"

"Because you were still trapped in the web of lies, Jason. You were still in the dark. Getting caught was like someone turning the lights on."

She's right. I see it now. It's so clear. So obvious. All those things I have been chasing after. They aren't the right things. And all the people I admire because they have those things, suddenly I don't admire them quite as much. Maybe they are caught in the web of lies too, only they can't see it. Nobody has turned the lights on for them yet.

Her metaphor works for me, and we start talking about all the places where I am plugged into this "web." Those connections are lines that tie me to my old identity. To my old life. To my old friend Porn Star. "You have to cut those cords, Jason," she tells me.

And we begin doing just that. One by one, Melissa helps me cut cords. And this is when I *really* start waking up. This is when everything turns upside down. The things I wanted so badly before, I no longer want. The things I valued so dearly, I no longer value. The people I admired so highly, I no longer admire. Everything gets reversed. At the risk of introducing too many metaphors, it is like the moment when Neo takes the little red pill in *The Matrix* and then learns that everything he thought was real is actually false.

As I look around my life, I see the lies everywhere. Ashley

Madison told me it was okay—even good!—to have an affair. But that's a lie. It is not okay to lie to my wife. It destroys my integrity and my marriage. But the people running Ashley Madison likely don't care about that, because they are making money.[3]

The porn industry labels itself as *entertainment*, but that's a lie. It is an industry that perpetuates the exploitation of women and is ruining our society's relationship with our natural sexuality. But the people running those companies don't care about these consequences, because they keep making money too.

My fancy sports car? Did it make me happy? No, that didn't work. Another lie. Suddenly it becomes a symbol of everything Porn Star stands for. He has an insatiable appetite for attention, and he wants a car that screams, "Look at me! Look at how successful I am! Give me attention!" I still don't know exactly what my future is, but I know enough by now to know that Porn Star is my past, and I want my family to be my future. That month I trade in my two-door sports car for a family sedan.

My mom, who has been supportively calling me every few days to check in and make sure I'm okay, challenges me on giving up the car.

"There's nothing wrong with having a nice car," she says. "You worked hard, and you earned it. You love that car."

She's right. There is nothing inherently wrong with having a sports car, but inside I know it is the right decision for *me*. I have to get rid of it. As I journal about it one morning, I realize why. It is because *intention* matters. My *intention* for having a fast car was to get attention and validation from society. I was using it to try to find happiness in external things. But now I'm learning that

---

3   Apparently helping people have affairs is big business. According to Wikipedia (https://en.wikipedia.org/wiki/Ashley_Madison), the website's membership reached 60 million in February 2019, and later that year a company executive boasted that their service "...helps create up to one million affairs every month."

none of the things the collective told me would make me happy will *actually* make me happy. It was all a lie. I stand firm in my resolve to replace my car.

Writing about intention somehow leads me to thinking about yoga, and I have another realization. My intention for doing yoga was to become healthy. In contrast, my intention for working out for the last twenty years had been to create a strong animal body that would be attractive to Anne Marie and other women. I had been working out to get attention from others, thinking it would make me happy, but it didn't. I was doing yoga to give attention to myself, and I felt great.

Do I need to make more money? Why? For what purpose? Because I can never have enough? This feels like a lie now, too.

"Would you rather have more money or spend more time with Anne Marie and be with Maya as she grows up?" Melissa asks in another call.

Again, the answer comes easily and is simple. "I want more time with Anne Marie and Maya." On that day I vow to stop traveling so much for work.

We continue cutting cords, and as we do, I see the same principle of subtraction from so many years ago return. I don't have to know exactly what my future will be, I just have to know which things from my past I'm going to let go of. Once I get rid of them, I will open space in my life for new things. Actually, this is already happening. The new things are SA. And yoga. And journaling. And reading self-help books. And drifting off to sleep listening to guided meditations at night. Over the last two months, *these* have become the rituals of my day. While SA gave me the original groundwork of clarity and direction, the consistent layering in of these other elements helps stabilize my identity and calm the emotional upheavals.

As I cut cords, my ego attachments weaken, and I move further away from my old life. I reach a point where Melissa, who is always pushing me, reminds me I cannot rest where I am. If I want to live a new, honest, and conscious life, I have to move forward and create it.

CHAPTER 13

"He lives a life exactly the opposite of most human lives.
He lives not to gratify his personal needs and wishes or his
physical appetites, but to hone himself into an efficient
spiritual machine, trained to bear the unbearable in the
service of the transpersonal goal."

—ROBERT MOORE AND DOUGLAS GILLETTE,
King Warrior Magician Lover

APRIL 2015

IT IS FIVE-THIRTY IN THE MORNING, STILL DARK OUTSIDE,
and I am sitting at the little kitchen table in my apartment. A
candle throws off just enough light for me to write in my journal
and see steam wafting up from my coffee cup. The only sounds
are the scratches of my pen as it moves across my notebook, and
an occasional light crackle from the flickering flame.

I have lived here for two months, and this is how I start every
day now. This place is my sanctuary. It is my home. Two months
may not sound like a long time, but for a guy who has never been

able to spend any significant time alone, it is an accomplishment. I am grateful for my daily rituals that keep me moving forward. In my little apartment, living my simple life, I feel more content than I have felt in decades.

Today I'm journaling about a conversation I had with Anne Marie on the phone last night. I see her briefly a few days a week now because one of her employees moved, and she needs to fill in the early shift on alternating days until she hires someone new. On those days I wake up at four thirty in the morning and go to our condo so she can go to work while I wait for Maya to wake up. When she does, I help her get ready, make her breakfast, and drop her off at school.

Despite the early hour, I cherish those mornings. I journal or do work at the kitchen table until Maya wakes up, and then I am fully present with her. More present than I have ever been with her before.

Yesterday when I arrived at the condo, I asked Anne Marie if she would like to talk and she agreed, promising to call me after Maya went to bed. Our call started off a little awkward. It was five or six weeks since we'd had a substantive conversation, and so much had happened, it was hard to know where to start or what to focus on. Eventually we started talking about a book Melissa assigned both of us to read a few weeks after I revealed my secrets: *Women Who Love Too Much* by Robin Norwood. The most impactful parts for us were the stories of how women who'd grown up with fathers who were addicts tended to enter relationships with other addicts as adults, which is exactly what had happened with us.

Anne Marie's father is a recovering alcohol and drug addict who had been sober for many years when all of this was happening. But during Anne Marie's childhood, he had significant struggles with his addictions. Anyone living with an addict knows that they are often not fully present. They might be physically absent while they engage in their addictive behavior, but even if they are in the room with you, they are often emotionally absent because they are so preoccupied with the internal battle of their addiction. Whatever the reasons, the child of an addict often grows up in a relationship with someone who is not fully emotionally present, and this begins to define what a relationship feels like for them. As they mature into adulthood, they are likely to be attracted to another person who is not fully emotionally present, because that is what they have learned as the normal feeling of a relationship.

For Anne Marie, I was the perfect fit. From the beginning of our relationship in college I had been very comfortable not being fully emotionally present. First, I had thrown myself into my college studies. Then I worked so much in the early days of my career that I didn't have much time for our relationship (recall that she moved to LA at one point because we barely saw each other anyway). When my work wasn't enough, I added porn, then philandering as other ways to distract my attention.

In her coaching sessions with Melissa, Anne Marie was learning how she had benefited from the situation we'd gotten into, and how she could have missed the signs that I was cheating for so many years. She wouldn't have been attracted to a guy that was fully emotionally present because it would have been uncomfortable for her to be fully emotionally vulnerable in return. On a subconscious level, my emotional distance was fine for her. It's what she was used to.

As she became consciously aware of this dynamic, she realized she had a choice to make: Did she want to continue co-creating with an addict?

"Why would I choose that for myself?" she asked me on the phone. It was painful for me to hear, but it was a fair question, and I didn't have an answer.

After we hung up, I sat hurting, staring at the floor for a long while. Waves of remorse washed over me. Then shame for all my lies. Then fears of losing Anne Marie came rushing back. Not just Anne Marie, but the future of what could have been our happy family. We'd been building our dream home—supposed to move into it in six months. We'd put enormous amounts of money, time, and energy into it, planning every detail. I'd visited the construction site almost every day for close to two years. That project was a symbol of Anne Marie and me building a new future together for us, and for our family. Now what? Were we just going to sell it to someone else for *their* family? Would Anne Marie and Maya move in and start a new life without me? My heart tore in two thinking I'd completely ruined our family's future.

I took a few deep breaths, knowing I had to let these feelings move through me. Then I reached for my journal and started writing the entry I am finishing this morning.

A few days ago, in an SA meeting, someone talked about the importance of surrendering. Not just surrendering and realizing we are powerless over our addictions, but surrendering in all areas of our lives where we experience pain or suffering. To learn when to say, "I can't control this," and then to let go, and have faith that the "river of life" (as he called it) would carry us safely.

Anne Marie was telling me that she wasn't sure we would stay together, and as I write I realize the least painful way to move forward is to surrender. I am already doing everything in my power to get well and to repair myself so I can enter into a healthy relationship with her, and if that isn't enough, there is nothing I can do about it. The only way for me to get well is to stay focused on my internal work.

* * *

IT IS ANOTHER WEDNESDAY MORNING, and again I'm on a call with Melissa. "Remember when we used to talk about your building having a cracked foundation?" she asks.

"Yes, I do."

"Well, that building has been completely smashed. It's gone now. Foundation and everything. Congratulations to you for getting to this point. It's time to go to the next level."

"I'm ready. Let's go."

"Okay," Melissa says. "Let's start climbing."

And this is when I begin "climbing my mountain." It is another metaphor she likes to use with her clients, and it becomes the basis for the next phase of my work with her.

It turns out the mountain she's referring to is my spiritual mountain. As we move deeper into the metaphor, I begin to understand that, up until this point in my life, I have been two-dimensional: I had a mind, and I had a body. I completely neglected to recognize the third dimension of myself: my spirit. Not knowing my spirit meant I didn't *really* know myself. No wonder I was looking for validation and attention from the outside world all this time. I was trying to fill what I thought was some kind of void inside myself. But that void wasn't a void at all, it was the real me, my spirit. It only felt like a void because I didn't know what it was.

I learn that if I get to know the real me, I won't feel a void inside anymore, and I won't keep looking outside myself for things to fill it. By realizing that I don't need more money, or fancy cars, or more women, I have already taken the smallest of steps in this direction. I feel happier and more at peace living my simple life of daily rituals than I have ever been.

From that moment, my sessions with Melissa take on an entirely new dimension. It is as if the last five years of coaching were only to lay the groundwork for this one, singular moment. The moment when I was ready to stop keeping secrets. The moment when all my interior walls came down, and Melissa could gain access to my entire psyche. She texts me every time she has a cancellation, and I take every session she can give me. Sometimes I have three or four sessions in a single week.

She assigns me YouTube videos to watch. Many are people I've never heard of before, but she wants me to spend time with them and hear their messages. So, while I'm eating meals in my tiny apartment, Caroline Myss tells me to stop complaining, take responsibility for my life, and grow up. Thich Nhat Hanh tells me to love myself and everyone on planet Earth. Brené Brown's messages about shame, vulnerability, and moving forward in the face of fear resonate deeply with me. Countless guests of Oprah reinforce the new vocabulary I am learning.

I climb, but it is a slow process. There are giant boulders blocking my path, and sometimes the only way around them is to crawl through a dark cave. I'm afraid of what I will find in those caves, but I put my trust in Melissa that she will help me through them.

In one session she asks me to think about one of my earliest childhood memories. I close my eyes and I'm immediately transported to the night when I was six years old, holding my knees on my bed, scared because I can hear my mom and Bill fighting in the hallway. I'm afraid my mom is really going to go drive off a cliff.

"Now as adult Jason, the Jason you are today, go into the room," she tells me.

I see myself enter the room.

"What do you want to tell little Jason?" she asks.

"I want to tell him that it's going to be okay."

"Go to him. Tell him."

I sit on the bed with little Jason, gather him into my arms, and I tell him it's going to be okay. He buries his head into my chest, and he cries. I cry too.

A week later we do the exercise again. This time I see little Jason when he is eleven years old. He lives in the new house in Hillsborough now. He is sitting in his room on his bed. His mom is in her dark room sleeping with a towel over her eyes. His step-father is at work. His sister is not home. He is sad that his mom is in bed all the time, and he's lonely. He feels like something isn't right, but he doesn't understand what. Again, I enter the room as adult Jason and sit next to him on the bed.

"Ask him what he wants to say," Melissa tells me.

I ask.

"I want to tell my mom to wake up," he says.

"Go tell her," I suggest to him.

He goes into his mom's room and tells her to wake up. He says it three times, but she doesn't move. He comes back into his room and sits on the bed next to me again.

"I don't understand," he says.

"Tell him his mom is very sick," Melissa instructs. "And it isn't his fault."

I tell him. He nods.

"What do you want to do with him?" Melissa asks.

"I want to take him outside, into the sunlight. I want to take him away from this place."

"So, take him."

I bring little Jason downstairs, help him put his jacket on, and we go outside into the sunlight. We play in the front yard. First soccer. Then we throw a baseball back and forth. After a while I ask him if he wants ice cream, and he says *yes*. Then I see the two of us walking down the street together, holding hands.

"When you are alone, Jason, you are never really alone," Melissa teaches me. "You are always with little Jason."

In the weeks that follow, little Jason's presence changes my life. I am no longer alone. He is always by my side. Perhaps more importantly, I am his guardian now. I am taking care of him. I realize that for my entire life I have really only been focused on myself. Caring for little Jason becomes the first selfless thing I do. I am in service to him now. I can't be confused and lost. He needs me to have courage and direction. More importantly, he needs me to be a role model for him.

As I write these things in my journal one morning, an old realization surfaces again, and hits me so hard I stop and stare at the page for a long while. *I need to grow up*, I've written. It is the same realization I had a year ago, but somehow it now takes on an entirely new meaning and a new level of depth. From that day forward, *I am ready to grow up* becomes one of the driving themes of my recovery.

* * *

I HAVEN'T EVEN THOUGHT ABOUT looking at porn since I revealed my secrets, which is the longest stretch I've gone in almost twenty years. My other sexual urges have continued to diminish, as well. And as the attention that I used to give those things frees up, my life somehow feels like it gets even simpler. The books I'm reading gradually drift from self-help into spiritual. One day Melissa jokes and tells me, "I'm not calling you Porn Star anymore. Now you are The Monk."

As I climb, Anne Marie climbs her mountain too. I have a rough sense of where she is because we've each given Melissa blanket permission to share anything that we talk about in our sessions. We still see each other a few mornings a week, but we aren't talking much, and the energy between us has changed. There is more distance. We are each climbing our own mountain, and it is deeply personal work. Being so separate from her still scares me a little, but it also feels right. It feels healthier. We already went through one untangling experience close to five years ago in San Francisco, and now we are untangling on an entirely new and much deeper level. I know we each have to follow the path of our own climb, even if those paths start to diverge.

As I journal about this, I remember lines that our marriage officiant included in our wedding vows twelve years earlier. They were borrowed from *The Prophet*, a book of twenty-six fables written by the Lebanese-American poet and writer Kahlil Gibran. When a student asks his Master about his thoughts on marriage, the Master acknowledges that couples will be together, and offers this advice:

But let there be spaces in your togetherness,
And let the winds of the heavens dance between you.
Love one another, but make not a bond of love:
Let it rather be a moving sea between the shores of your souls.
Fill each other's cup but drink not from one cup.
Give one another of your bread but eat not from the same loaf.
Sing and dance together and be joyous, but let each one
of you be alone,
Even as the strings of a lute are alone though they quiver

with the same music.

Give your hearts, but not into each other's keeping. For only the hand of Life can contain your hearts.

And stand together yet not too near together. For the pillars of the temple stand apart. And the oak tree and the cypress grow not in each other's shadow.

It is the message of the last line that is most memorable for me: the oak and the cypress can't grow if they are too close together. Anne Marie and I, we are those trees. We need more space between us so we can each grow. Instead of focusing so much on our relationship and the question of marriage versus divorce, we each have to focus on our own personal growth and healing; on climbing our own mountains. If we just focus on that, then we will both grow into strong trees, and then it won't matter if we stay together or get divorced.

More time passes, and I keep working the SA steps. I keep journaling. I keep doing yoga. I spend more time with little Jason. I visit him in his past, or I take him for walks in nature in the present. Gradually he is growing up, and he is more like a young man now than the boy he was when I first met him. I read more spiritual books. I am climbing.

In my sessions with Melissa, she pulls me further up the mountain, and I try not to slide all the way back down to where we started between our phone calls. It is slow work, and it is exhausting, but gradually I'm gaining ground. A few steps at a time, I am making progress.

In what would become one of the most memorable coaching sessions of my life, one day Melissa senses that it would help if I could feel what it's like higher up on the mountain. To feel the sun warm my face up there. To smell the fresh air. To experience the simplicity of a life lived with deep responsibility and integrity. Not just integrity in terms of telling the truth, but also the integrity that comes from knowing yourself fully. From integrating your body, mind, spirit, and all of your fragmented identities into one, whole person. It is important so that I have an idea of where I'm heading with all this hard work and climbing.

I sit on the edge of the small couch in my apartment, back straight, my feet firmly on the floor. I close my eyes, lift my head, and we start ascending. It is part coaching, part guided meditation. I don't know how she does it, but at some point, I see and feel myself rising above the clouds. I see the top of my mountain far above me, and, as I look around, I notice I'm in a mountain range that extends as far as I can see in every direction. Thousands of tall peaks reaching toward the sky. I instinctively know that each peak represents a person. Everyone has their own spiritual mountain to climb.

The air is fresh and pure, and I take in a deep breath. The sun is on my skin, and suddenly my body is enveloped by a warmth I can't explain. And then I notice that the sun isn't the sun; it is just a bright light in the sky. I am drawn to the light, and as I focus on it a sense of peace washes over my body. It is like nothing I have ever felt before. It is ineffable. A sense of total completeness. Here, I need nothing. Here, is everything. Tears stream down my face. I realize that Melissa has barely been talking for several minutes now. I am on some kind of journey of my own.

"How do you feel?" she eventually asks, quietly.

"I can't describe it. I feel perfect. Everything is perfect."

I bathe in the light, and I soak in the feelings. We are quiet for several more minutes.

"Welcome to the other side," she says.

* * *

ANOTHER MONTH TICKS BY, AND summer approaches, with its promise of warm sunshine and longer days. My rituals remain the same, and my intensity doesn't waver. With Melissa's help, I actively seek out every dark cave I can find on my mountain and crawl through them. My sessions are raw and often involve significant tears. She helps me hold up a mirror and look at every part of myself, whether I like what I see or I not. The only way for me to really change is to see and accept the parts of myself that I don't like; no, that I loathe. I need to have compassion for those parts of myself, and then for myself as a whole. I need to love myself completely. Only then will I be prepared to enter a loving relationship with Anne Marie (or anyone).

At SA meetings, I get more comfortable sharing my story and my thoughts about my recovery. I grow to love and trust the people in the groups I attend, and I feel their love and acceptance and understanding in return. I begin to celebrate longer sobriety milestones, but when I do, I no longer feel proud. Each milestone is a reminder that the only way to reach the next one is to stay humble and continue living a simple life with integrity.

I still see Anne Marie a few mornings a week, and lately I've noticed that our interactions, while brief, are warmer. One morning after I drop Maya off at school, I stop by her juice shop and ask if she and Maya would like to come over for dinner one night, and she accepts my invitation. As I drive back to my apartment that morning, I feel like I'm seeing a bright sunny morning for the first time in my life. Something has switched inside me. I'm seeing the world through new eyes. I am no longer that guy who was lying and cheating and sneaking around. I'm not looking at porn or hookup websites and scheming and plotting rendezvous. I am living a simple and disciplined life. I am living with integrity.

I wake up early every day, and from sunrise to sunset everything I do is to nourish myself, to nourish my soul. At night I fall asleep peacefully and have restful sleep. I still battle occasional urges to masturbate, but I no longer see these moments as failures; they are just another part of my climb, or a clue to an entry point for deeper work with Melissa.

I am honest about my story and my life, with myself and with everyone. Eventually I share what I'm going through with several young male CEOs whom I work with most closely, as a sort of cautionary tale of what *not* to do. I turn on the lights for them, and they are entranced by the story. Every time I share it—every time I take ownership of it and acknowledge it but don't judge it—it gives me more strength.

My life is so much simpler now. More transparent. More honest. More peaceful. The morning I extend the invitation to Anne Marie, I can see the person I am becoming and the new life that will unfold in front of me if I stay humble and keep climbing. It feels great.

* * *

THE NIGHT ARRIVES FOR ANNE Marie and Maya to join me for dinner. As I greet them at the door, Maya, in a flowery dress, excitedly thrusts a white box in my hands.

"We brought cookies for dessert!" she announces. I give her a hug and then look up at Anne Marie, who gives me a warm smile.

We have all dressed up for the occasion, and it feels like a little family reunion.

Maya races into my apartment and immediately discovers the stairs leading up to the loft bedroom. She makes her way halfway up and then turns around to survey the little space. "Is this where you've been working on your big project, Daddy?" she asks. Unsure, I look over at Anne Marie, who offers a nod.

"Yes." My eyes stay locked on Anne Marie's. "It's been a big project, but I think it's going to turn out really good." Anne Marie and I both laugh a little.

I fret over every detail of dinner to make sure it is a great meal. Despite everything that's happened and not talking much for several months, spending time together is somehow easy for me and Anne Marie. We have changed. We are healthier individuals, with less agenda on each other. We aren't all tangled up anymore. The energy between us is cleaner. Easier. Lighter.

We begin seeing each other more frequently. I stop by the juice shop occasionally just to say *hi*. Then we get coffees together. Then lunch. She shares how much she has learned about herself and our relationship in the months of intensive self-reflection. She understands the choice that is before her now very clearly, and she is prepared to set healthier boundaries for herself.

Her expectations are clear: If I stop climbing for even a moment, we will get divorced. She sees and hears (through Melissa) how much I have changed in a relatively short period. She also takes responsibility for her role in what happened and doesn't just point a finger at me and say it was all my fault. But the wound is still raw, and it will be a long time before I regain her trust completely. She isn't even sure if that will *ever* happen. I understand. By this point I've learned that I don't have control over if or how much she will trust me in the future. The only thing

I have control over is how hard I'm climbing my mountain, and so that remains the only thing I focus on.

* * *

FOR SEVERAL YEARS IN A row, our family visited a dude ranch in the summer. The trip has become a small tradition for us. The ranch is popular, and deposits must be paid six months in advance, so there was no way to cancel the trip for this year after our ordeal started. But this summer Anne Marie doesn't want to go on vacation together. If she is going to take a vacation, she wants to go somewhere alone. I've been living alone and focusing almost 100 percent of my time and energy on my personal growth and recovery, but she hasn't had that luxury because she is building a small business while essentially being a single parent to Maya.

I understand that she needs time alone to rest. And to nourish herself. And to sort through her feelings and think about the path she wants to take forward. So we make separate travel arrangements. As Maya and I board our plane for the dude ranch, Anne Marie waves goodbye from the gate. She is heading to a spiritual retreat center near Los Angeles, and her flight departs shortly after ours.

I have a wonderful time with Maya at the dude ranch that week. It is a very special bonding experience, especially since I hadn't seen her much the last four months. Plus, I am a new person now, and even more present with her. I have no cell service and Anne Marie isn't using her phone at her retreat center, so the two of us have zero contact with each other that week.

As fate would have it, I get a text message from the landlord of my apartment when Maya and I land back in Salt Lake City: a water pipe has burst in the unit above mine. The damage is so severe that I have to move into another unit, but they're having trouble finding a vacant one, so they offer to reimburse me if I need to find a hotel room. Anne Marie isn't returning until tomorrow, so I figure she won't mind if I spend the night at our condo. Maya and I head straight for my apartment to check on the damage and gather whatever things I need to salvage or have for the next few days.

The following afternoon, Maya and I drive to the airport to pick Anne Marie up. As I park the car and we start walking toward baggage claim, I get butterflies in my stomach. Anne Marie and I haven't spoken at all for a week, and aside from a few recent coffees and lunches, really haven't spoken to each other much for several months. While I'm waiting for her at baggage claim I get the same feelings I had when I waited for her to exit her Economics classroom way back in college. I am giddy and excited to see her.

As she comes down the escalator, our eyes meet, and we smile at each other as Maya jumps up and down with excitement. Anne Marie looks rested and refreshed, her skin kissed gently by the sun. We hug for a long time and don't say much. Whatever we are feeling goes far beyond words.

We hold hands the entire car ride home, and excitedly catch up with each other as Maya dozes peacefully in her car seat in the back. I tell her about the week at the dude ranch, and she tells me all about her amazing week on retreat.

"Oh, and this is interesting," I start as we get closer to Park City. "My condo unit got severely water damaged last night. Something about a broken pipe in the unit above mine. I stayed in the downstairs bedroom last night. Would it be okay if I stay there again tonight? I think my landlord is lining up a temporary unit I can move into tomorrow."

Anne Marie is quiet for a minute. "Yes, of course," she finally says. "You are welcome to stay." I look at her, and she smiles at me and squeezes my hand.

That night after she bathes Maya and puts her to bed, we sit up talking for hours. We share more details of the past week, and then share more of the insights and realizations we've had over the prior months. On the outside we're still the same humans of Jason and Anne Marie, but on the inside, we are changing—and had changed—into two completely new people. If we move forward together from here it will be in a totally new relationship. A new marriage. The next morning, she invites me to move back into the condo.

* * *

THAT DAY, AFTER I DROP Maya off at school, I go over to my apartment and pack my things. The place is a water-damaged mess, and the remediation crew has already stacked most of my belongings in a pile in the living room. As I make trips of stuff out to my car, walking the hallways these final times, I notice hints of sadness move through my body. I will miss this place. It was my haven. My refuge. My cocoon. It was small and it was safe, and I have so much appreciation for what it provided me. Inside these walls, alone with nothing but my simple daily rituals and the guidance of wise teachers, I changed. I cut the cords that were keeping me tied to an old life of distractions and deceit. I looked inward and plumbed the depths of my soul. I began integrating my mind, my body, and my spirit into a more unified whole.

As I make my last sweep of the place, I duck into the bathroom to make sure I haven't left anything in the cabinets. After I close the last one, I stand up, and my image in the mirror catches my attention. I stand up straight, and I look at myself. For a long time, I couldn't look at myself in the mirror, but these days I can.

I continue making eye contact with myself until I *see* myself. I look different than I did four months ago. I look relaxed. At peace. When I arrived here, I was lost. I was running. I was scared. But I went through violent emotional storms, and I survived. I crawled through dark caves, and I survived. I am wiser now. I am maturing. When I look in the mirror, I no longer see a scared boy. I see a man. A man who is not running from his feelings anymore. A man who is not hiding. A man who is taking responsibility for his actions. A man who is ready to be a husband. Ready to be a father. When I look at myself, I see a man who is finally living with integrity.

I smile at the man in the mirror. He is my friend, and I like him. No, I love him. Then I turn off the lights and I lock up the apartment. He and I have a mountain to go climb.

THE END

AFTERWORD

"For me, writing is an act of reciprocity with the world. It's what I can give back in return for everything that has been given to me."

—ROBIN WALL KIMMERER, *Braiding Sweetgrass*

FEBRUARY 2022

IT IS SEVEN YEARS SINCE THE DAY I GOT MY WAKE-UP CALL. So much has happened since then.

Anne Marie and I are still married, and our relationship is deeper, happier, and more fulfilling than ever. In *The Seat of the Soul*, a book I read in the summer of 2017, author Gary Zukav suggests that a successful modern marriage will be a spiritual partnership based on a joint commitment to (1) engage in a continuous, never-ending process of spiritual growth, and (2) support the other partner in their spiritual growth. I agree with him completely.

Anne Marie and I keep changing through our commitment to continuous growth. We keep becoming new people. By extension, our partnership keeps evolving. This constant evolution means we approach every day as the beginning of a new life together, which has created a vibrancy in our relationship that we cherish.

We completed our construction project and moved into our new home shortly after I returned to our condo to live with her and Maya. The following year, we welcomed a son into our family, Milo. The new house, and our new family, have been a fresh new start for us. A new foundation to build on. Our home is bright, with lots of windows, and reflects our internal goal of always trying to live in the light.

To support that, we make great efforts to keep our life simple. We are raising two beautiful children together, and we could not be more proud of them. We take our parenting roles seriously and believe it is our responsibility to help guide these two humans into the world with as much light in them as possible. It is a full-time job and our highest priority.

Both of us have continued our coaching work with Melissa, who remains a shining star in our lives. She is extraordinary. I think what makes her so effective is that she, herself, has never stopped climbing her unique spiritual mountain, and she climbs with more vigor and intensity than any of her clients. That is how she stays far out ahead of us.

I believe modern life is complex and that everyone should have someone they can talk to openly and honestly, with no secrets. It can be a therapist, coach, or mentor—it doesn't matter what you call them—what's important is that you have a person you can talk to who isn't your spouse or your parent or your friend. Someone who can hold you accountable in ways those other people can't. Someone who will call you out on your bullshit from a place of love for you, without fear that you will reject them for being honest (as most friends and family typically are). The most important thing to look for in this person, in my opinion, is a commitment to their own continued growth. If it feels like they hold an attitude that suggests they have completed their climb, that should be a cause for concern.

I realize I've lived a privileged life since I was born, and not everyone can afford to have a life coach on speed dial. I hope that by sharing my story openly, through this book and in follow-up conversations, I can "open source" much of what I learned from Melissa so that others can benefit from her wisdom as well.

* * *

ONCE I REVEALED MY SECRETS, it took me years to come to terms with the guilt and shame I kept inside. *Healing the Shame That Binds You*, by John Bradshaw, was an important book for me when I read it in the spring of 2018. It helped me identify those feelings still lurking inside, so I could finally begin to let them go. I have learned to accept my past as part of my journey and to appreciate everything it has taught me.

To be clear, sharing my story is not an attempt to justify my choices and past actions. I take full responsibility for everything I have done, and I apologize sincerely to any women I exploited while I was engaged in my bad behavior. After years of reflection, I understand that all my experiences have shaped me into the person who is now writing these words. I am proud of the man I have become, even if I'm not proud of how I got here.

I am grateful that I got caught and was forced to find myself at such a young age, yet I harbor no false beliefs that my climb is somehow over. I went over two years without even thinking about pornography, but then one day there was a distant urge.

Over time it grew, until one day I found myself in that place again. Fortunately, by then, I understood that my vice was my teacher. It was a sort of "canary in the coal mine," an early warning system telling me that something wasn't right in my life. Maybe there was something I was in resistance to. Maybe there was a truth about the world, another person, or myself that I didn't want to accept. With reflection and journaling, coaching with Melissa, and conversations with Anne Marie, my vice has become an entry point for me to explore deeper and deeper into my soul, to understand all its intricate facets, and most importantly, to love and accept all of them. Over the years, this constant exploration and polishing helped me integrate more and more pieces of myself, and the energy around my vice has continued to dissipate.

* * *

MY JOURNEY INVOLVES AN ADDICTION to pornography and sex, but those are just the details of my story. Really it is a universal story of pain, and self-medicating, and trying to escape. So many of us have stories like this.

The pain of my story evolves out of my early childhood experiences of losing my father and then losing my mother to her depression. But I want to be clear that I don't think my behavior as an adult is their "fault" or that they were bad parents. They were doing the best they could with the cards life dealt them, just like the rest of us.

Today, I have a lot of compassion for my mother. She wasn't well, but nobody knew how to help her or give her the tools to know how to help herself. She inherited her depression from her own childhood traumas. Bill had his own childhood traumas that drove his anger. My dad had his. Anne Marie's parents had theirs. None of them are bad people; they were just carrying forward the traumas of their past. The more Anne Marie and I understand this, the more we want to break that cycle for our ancestral lines. Doing this requires both of us to grow up, step forward, and each take responsibility for everything that happens to us individually. And we are trying to do this for our children too, by creating a family environment of light and consciousness that encourages them to take deep levels of personal responsibility.

* * *

THE WORD INTEGRITY HAS TWO meanings:[4]

The quality of being honest and having strong moral principles; moral uprightness.

The state of being whole and undivided.

Most people focus on the first meaning of the word. Over time I have come to appreciate the second definition just as much, if not more than the first.

At some point in my life, I had neither of these things. I had no integrity. After my secrets were revealed, becoming honest with myself and everyone else was relatively easy compared to becoming a whole, undivided person. Becoming honest just meant I had to stop keeping secrets. Becoming whole is a constant process of looking deeper inside myself, finding holes and the missing pieces to fill them. At first, the holes and pieces are like huge boulders,

---

4   Definitions from Oxford Languages.

easy to identify and to work on. But over time, after the biggest pieces have been put back into place, it is more challenging to see the smaller pieces. It becomes slow and painstaking work that requires patience and perseverance. This is what my climb is like today.

As I've continued becoming more whole—having more integrity—I have grown in love for myself which, interestingly, has led me to grow in love for others and for the world around me. When I was a young man, I saw myself as an individual entity that needed to acquire money and power and other external sources of validation to be secure in the world. To feel safe. Now my security comes from inside myself, and my validation comes from knowing who I am more deeply and more completely. Other people are no longer threats because they might take something I want, nor are they pawns in a game I'm playing. They are humans trying to figure out their way in this world, just like me. We are all the same. We are brothers and sisters, and we are all in this together.

Instead of feeling like an individual entity that needs to take for me, I now feel like a tiny piece of a collective humanity that thrives when we all share with each other. I no longer want to take from humanity. I want to give and to be in service. I view writing this book as my first significant act of service.

We don't have to figure everything out ourselves. We should share our stories so we can learn from each other. My hope is that by sharing my story, other young men can avoid some of the pitfalls I fell into. I also hope that, for anyone who feels trapped in a dark place, my story offers a beacon of hope that you can change. You can find the light again.

* * *

SO OFTEN WE DON'T TALK about our secrets or face them honestly because we judge ourselves or are afraid of being judged by others. But ironically, it is our secrets that keep us sick. Worse still, we bury our truths with behaviors that cause even more pain to ourselves and to others.

It was Melissa's love and willingness to not judge me—to be curious about my behavior—that encouraged me to finally open up. She and Anne Marie both held a nonjudgmental space for me. They understood that my experiences were part of my soul's journey, that I was learning something, and that I needed space and time to figure out what those lessons were and to learn them. Opening up—telling the truth—is what finally started my growth. My true healing. Then, as I healed my wounds, I stopped hurting myself. And as I stopped hurting myself, I stopped hurting others.

There is so much more I want to say, but perhaps this is enough for our first meeting. Thank you for reading this book. I wish you luck on your journey. Don't be afraid to tell your secrets. Most importantly, don't stop climbing.

ACKNOWLEDGMENTS

WRITING THIS BOOK WAS THE MOST DIFFICULT THING I'VE ever done, and also the most rewarding.

To Anne Marie: My love. My best friend. There is no question I have that you can't answer in a way that elevates my consciousness. Holding myself to the standard of a partner you deserve gives me direction in the toughest parts of my climb. Thank you for holding space for me. Thank you for taking care of the kids and putting your life on hold so I could make time to write this story. Thank you for your supportive words when I feared I would never finish. Thank you for reading all the drafts and giving your honest feedback. This book is as much yours as it is mine.

To Maya: My daughter. My friend. You held your mom and I together at two very important crossroads. Wanting to be a good father for you helped give me the courage to really change. I love you with all my heart, and I have so much to thank you for.

To Milo: My son. My buddy. Thank you for slowing down time, pulling me deeper into the present moment, and giving my life a richness and purpose I didn't know before. I love you dearly.

To Melissa: Life coach. Spiritual guide. Seer. Knower. I owe my life to you. When I was lost and alone, you soaked me in love, and showed me the way. No words can express the depth of gratitude I hold in my soul for what you've done for me.

To Stephanie: You are the best business partner anyone could have. Thank you for holding down all the forts so I could stay focused on creating this book.

To Sham: My brother across the pond. Your encouragement was the push that finally got me writing. Thank you for believing in me.

To my parents, Carolyn, Bill, and Norman: Thank you for caring for me, and for giving me the opportunities and experiences that launched me into the world. I love you all very much.

To Steve and Cathy: This book would not have happened without your love and support. Thank you for taking care of our family so I could sequester myself and write.

To Lisa: My Scribe. My editor. And now my friend. Thank you for teaching me so much about the craft of writing. Most of all, thank you for always pushing me out of my comfort zone.

A special thanks to all my beta readers: Jenny, Tara, Rich, Brad, Daniel, Sham, and Anne Marie. This book would not be half as good without your thoughtful insights. Thank you for your time, attention, and dedication to my project.

Thank you, Nicole, for creating a beautiful cover for the book. It was such a pleasure to work with you.

Last, but certainly not least, a very big THANK YOU to my amazing team at Scribe, especially Mikey and Katie. Thank you for keeping me focused and saving me from myself. You guys are pure professionals.

ABOUT THE AUTHOR

ENTREPRENEUR, VENTURE CAPITALIST, AND AUTHOR
Jason Portnoy began his career at PayPal, working closely with
technology icons like Peter Thiel, Elon Musk, Max Levchin, and
Reid Hoffman. He served as the first Chief Financial Officer of
Palantir Technologies (NYSE: PLTR) and later founded Oakhouse
Partners, a top-performing venture capital firm.

Jason is sought after as a trusted advisor to technology company CEOs and has spoken on topics ranging from executive lead-
ership to the intersections of technology and humanity. He holds
engineering degrees from both Stanford University (MS) and the
University of Colorado (BS), and he currently lives in Park City,
Utah, with his wife, two children, and their family dog.

To learn more or to contact Jason please visit
www.jasonportnoy.com.

Made in the USA
Coppell, TX
16 December 2022

89621537R00129